To My Future
ASSISTANT

To My Future
ASSISTANT

Your Foolproof Guide to Dealing with the Boss From Hell

LYDIA WHITLOCK

SPHERE

First published in Great Britain in 2013 by Sphere

First published in the United States by Three Rivers Press,
an imprint of the Crown Publishing Group,
a division of Random House, Inc., New York

Portions of this work first appeared on the author's blog,
ToMyAssistant.com

A CIP catalogue record for this book
is available from the British Library.

ISBN 978-0-7515-5276-8

Typeset in Versailles by M Rules
Printed and bound in Great Britain by
Clays Ltd, St Ives plc

Papers used by Sphere are from well-managed forests
and other responsible sources.

MIX
Paper from
responsible sources
FSC® C104740

Sphere
An imprint of
Little, Brown Book Group
100 Victoria Embankment
London EC4Y 0DY

An Hachette UK Company
www.hachette.co.uk

www.littlebrown.co.uk

To my parents, Meg and Mick Whitlock, who helped me build the skills to get a terrible job and the confidence to leave it.

CONTENTS

AUTHOR'S NOTE

The situations put forth in this book are not based on specific jobs I've had or bosses I've known, but on the common assistant experience. Had most of these things actually happened to me, I'm not sure I'd be alive to write about them.

PLEASE ALLOW ME TO INTRODUCE MYSELF

To My Future Assistant:

It's me, your boss. Well, I'm not actually your boss yet. But I will be someday, when I'm finally rich and powerful enough to hire you. (Let's just both agree to work from the assumption that I will actually be rich and powerful one day and leave it at that.)

For now, I'm still an assistant, sitting in her cubicle, waiting for the day to finally end, just like you are, though I imagine your computer is a little faster, your mobile phone a little smaller, and your car a little more airborne. Just kidding! We both know you could never afford a flying car on your salary.

I'd like to think that I haven't changed that much between now and whenever it is you're reading this: that I still have a sense of humor about this business and about myself, that I can carry on an extended conversation about topics that aren't directly related to what I do for a living, that I still have a basic understanding of how computers work, and that I haven't gained too much weight from secretly stress-eating fast food in my car to fill the hunger left by eating only small and expensive salads in front of my coworkers.

But I know how this goes. One minute I'm commiserating with fellow assistants at happy hour, the next I'm putting £15 sushi boxes that I won't even eat on my Platinum AMEX and keeping the receipt so I can expense them. It's an uncommon person who survives the journey up the food chain with both personality and principles intact, and while I'd like to think that highly of myself, I know better.

So, dear future assistant, here's your safety net and survival guide in one. Here are all the things I will never do to you, but which many of your other bosses probably will. And when I inevitably slip up and let my job get the best of my temper and my sanity, well, you are more than welcome to wave this list in my face.

Right after you bring me a cup of coffee. Black. No sugar. Thanks.

Your Future Boss

1

LIFE *at the* OFFICE

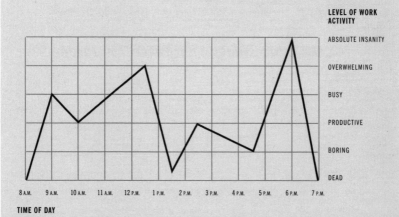

LEVEL OF WORK ACTIVITY

ABSOLUTE INSANITY

OVERWHELMING

BUSY

PRODUCTIVE

BORING

DEAD

8 A.M.   9 A.M.   10 A.M.   11 A.M.   12 P.M.   1 P.M.   2 P.M.   3 P.M.   4 P.M.   5 P.M.   6 P.M.   7 P.M.

TIME OF DAY

EVERY SINGLE DAY

All the Little Things That Drive You Insane

6%

SUBSTANTIVE, IMPORTANT WORK that contributes to your professional development and teaches you valuable information

12%

LOOKING FOR A NEW JOB while fantasizing about winning the lottery

34%

ANSWERING THE PHONE and **RETURNING E-MAILS**

14%

BROWSING THE INTERNET, because there is nothing else to do

14%

NODDING ATTENTIVELY while I talk

20%

SCHEDULING MY LIFE

YOUR TIME AT THE OFFICE
A Breakdown

15%
PLOTTING
how to take down my competitors and get promoted

20%
AVOIDING PHONE CALLS
I don't want to take

12%
BEGRUDGINGLY TAKING PHONE CALLS and ATTENDING MEETINGS

15%
AVOIDING MEETINGS
I don't want to attend

18%
MAKING CALLS
to people who will never call me back

20%
FACEBOOK

MY TIME AT THE OFFICE
A Breakdown

Quadrupling Your Workload
(Unnecessarily)

I will not tear confidential documents into many small and irregularly sized pieces before handing them to you to shred, one by one.

Dictation *(Repetitive)*

If I ever ask you to take dictation, it will be when I don't already have something written down. I will not make you come into my office and try to keep up while I read aloud from a set of notes I already put on paper but refuse to just hand to you, because I enjoy hearing the sound of my own voice and think my thoughts are magnificent when read out loud in a dramatic tone.

Clothing *(Yours)*

When you come into work dressed well, I won't say, "You look nice. Do you have an interview?"

Office Celebrations
(Exclusions)

I will not make you sit at your desk and answer my phones while everyone in the office (including myself) enjoys cake and ice cream in the conference room to celebrate someone's birthday.

Decorations *(Mandatory)*

I will not make you hang my child's crayon drawings of you above your desk, rather than the list of important phone numbers you refer to on an hourly basis, especially if those drawings imply that you have four chins.

Projects *(Revisions)*

When you're working on a project and bring me a first draft, I will not make a single revision and hand it back to you, causing you to think there was only one thing wrong with it, and then repeat this action fifty times over a span of four hours, taking you on an emotional roller-coaster ride by repeatedly flummoxing your hopes that the draft you just gave me was the last.

Brevity (Excessive)

I will not ask you to write me a summary of a Wikipedia article.

Anger (Mine)

When I'm angry at a person or situation, I won't expect you to be as upset about it as I am. I will expect you to be the less crazy person in our working relationship, not a pandering sycophant who only fuels the flames of my emotional outbursts. When you remain calm and helpful throughout one of my fits of pique, I'll appreciate it instead of turning my anger toward you for being "too cool for school."

The Conference Room
(Making Up My Mind)

When you ask me if you should book the conference room for a meeting that's two weeks away, and I say, "Nah. I'll do it in my office," that means I will actually be taking the meeting in my office, not telling you ten minutes beforehand that "you should have booked the conference room anyway, because you know how messy my office gets sometimes!"

Permission (Unnecessary)

I will not make you ask me if you can go to the bathroom, as if I'm your primary school teacher. I'll trust that you can accurately judge when you can slip away for a few minutes without the whole world collapsing around me while you're gone.

Technology (Social Networking)

I will not call you into my office in a serious tone of voice, tell you to close the door, and then ask, in a whisper, "How do I untag myself from this Facebook picture?"

Feedback (Ambiguous)

When asked for my opinion on a project you turned in, I will not respond by shrugging and saying, "It is what it is . . ."

Your Birthday *(Judgments)*

If our company cracks open a bottle of champagne for every office birthday, I will not raise an eyebrow and mutter, "Had enough yet?" when you go back for a second glass on your own birthday.

Highlighting *(Excessive)*

I will not have you highlight parts of a document for me, type the highlighted parts into an e-mail and send it to me, and then have you read that e-mail to me over the phone as I drive to lunch, because I didn't have time to look at what you just spent the past forty-five minutes coloring yellow and then retyping.

The Internet *(Learning About)*

I will not make you write a one-page memo explaining the origin and history of an Internet meme that the president of our company made a brief reference to during our last staff meeting.

Storage *(Not the Primary Function of Your Desk)*

I will not regularly leave random documents and items on your desk, covering the things you're actually working on, and expect them to be in the exact same place when I need them again in four hours.

Criticism *(Odd)*

I will not tell you to stop crossing your arms "because it makes you look angry."

Noise Pollution *(Hypocritical)*

I will not loudly and atonally hum Top 40 hits whenever I'm not speaking to someone on the phone or in person, but then yell at you from my office to "cut out that racket" when you're gently tapping your foot while working on a time-sensitive and stressful project.

Disaster Areas *(Causes of)*

I will not tell you to "clean up your desk—it's a disaster," when the reason for its looking so messy is that you're trying to organize the two-foot-high stack of random papers I dumped on the corner of it earlier that morning, with only the word "Here."

Jokes *(Reduced, Recycled, and Reused)*

Every time you come into work dressed in black, which happens at least once a week, I will not loudly ask you, "Who died?!" and expect you to laugh with me at my hilariously original joke.

Responsibilities *(Unwanted)*

If our office allows dogs, I will not regularly bring mine to work and put you in charge of cleaning up after it when it pees everywhere. (Its favorite spot to pee will be under your desk, because that's just how things work.)

Alerts *(Pointless)*

I will not make you set up a Google Alert for my name, so that you have to sift through hundreds of e-mails every morning about the four thousand other people with my name in the country, all of whom are more famous than I, and then tell me yet again that no, I am not "in the news."

Cleaning Up After Myself *(I Am Not a Dog)*

I will not ask to borrow your "office sweater," which you keep around due to the extreme temperatures of our central air system, and return it to you at the end of the day covered in my hair, which is very clearly a different color and length than yours.

Compliments

When I compliment you on a job well done, and you reply, "Thank you!" with a pleased but not overly proud smile on your face, I will not take it as an opportunity to lecture you about how you shouldn't let your head get too big—after all, "you didn't do that good a job."

Pointing *(Rather Than Smearing)*

When you're trying to show me something on your computer screen, I will not press my fingers against it to indicate where I want you to look, causing you to have to clean the grease off your screen three times as often as anyone else in the office. I will point without touching things, like a normal person.

Visibility *(Importance of)*

If we sit out of each other's line of sight, I will not regularly hold up something (invisible to you) and shout, "What do you think of this?!" forcing you to sprint to my office in order to give me a prompt response. Instead, I will just calmly ask you to please come into my office and take a look at something.

Feedback *(Traps)*

I will not ask you how I did during a presentation and tell you

to "answer honestly," when you know from experience that if you say I did well, I will accuse you of being a sycophant, and if you gently say it could have maybe gone better, I will not speak to you for the rest of the day or probably even the week.

Mispronunciation *(Insistence on)*

I will not mispronounce a common word so egregiously that even my colleagues laugh about it behind my back, yet rebuff every subtle attempt you make to get me to pronounce it correctly, insisting that you are the one who's saying it wrong.

Staring *(Discomforting)*

If we share an office, I will not pick an area just above and to the right of your head to stare at when I'm "thinking." I will instead choose a patch of air that doesn't make you think that I'm staring either at you or at someone invisible behind you.

Greetings
(Unsettling Responses to)

I will not respond to your cheerful "Good morning!" with a raised eyebrow and a sneer, making you think that you've already done something wrong by 9:05 A.M.

Impossible Requests
(Repeated)

I will not ask you on a near-weekly basis to edit a pdf for me and then, every time you let me know that you'll need a Word document to do that, get just as frustrated as the last time and question your usefulness as an assistant yet again.

Disorganization
(Achieving New Levels of)

I will not call you into my office at least once a week to ask you to help me find a computer file that I have saved in five different locations, each of which is a different version, none of which is the version I want, because I accidentally deleted that one.

BOSS VOCABULARY 101

Like a damaged gene that causes vagueness and passive-aggressive behavior, there is a certain vocabulary passed down from boss to assistant, due to a belief that sounding like the boss is the next best thing to being the boss. Well, it's not. Below are some terms to avoid if you want to stop the vicious cycle:

challenge *(n)* Typically said in an enticing tone of voice; anything described as such is really just a tedious and difficult project in disguise as a way to impress the boss. Which it won't.

Example: "I have a challenge for you! I need you to sort these two years of credit card receipts by date before I send them to my accountant, because even though it's my accountant's job to do so, I value his time much more than I value yours!"

Internet, the *(n)* A blanket word used by bosses to describe anything having to do with Internet connectivity or even just basic technology, from e-mail to IMs to YouTube to mobile phone service.

Example: "The Internet is broken. Call IT and tell them that. Yes, in my exact words."

Let's . . . *(v)* The beginning of a sentence spoken by the boss who wants to tell you to do something but is too passive-aggressive to actually give you a direct order and therefore starts everything with the incorrect suggestion that both of you will be performing the task.

Example: Most annoyingly found in the sentence "Let's order lunch," when the lunch order is just for one and no offers were made to extend it to two.

my office *(n)* Words that the boss will use to refer to you, rather than using your name, both as a way to show peers that he or she is important enough to have an assistant and to show you that he or she owns your ass.

Example: "My office will handle . . ." Usually referring to a meeting or phone call of which you were completely unaware before you were told you'd be "handling" it.

Related: **handle** *(v)* A word used by bosses to let their colleagues know that their assistant will be taking charge of a task, whether it's scheduling a meeting, typing up notes from a call, conferencing fifteen people together on the phone at 8:30 A.M., or driving all over town to buy a bunch of stupid gag gifts for a meeting. Bosses typically use this word for two reasons: first, because they always prefer to type one word in place of more than one, and second, because it allows them to give no more instructions than that one word. The assistant who asks for further instructions will likely be told three words: "Just handle it."

political *(adj)* A word used to describe any situation that the boss is too lazy/scared to deal with.

Example: "Well, I'd love for you to get a pay rise, but I'm afraid it's just too political for me to ask at this time."

thanks *(n)* A word used by bosses when they realize their assistants are almost at the breaking point, in an attempt to make them feel appreciated for just a little bit longer so as much work as possible can be sucked out of them before they're allowed to go home at 9 P.M.

Example: Every utterance of the word *thanks* by every boss ever.

20%

UNSETTLING PERSONAL DOCUMENTS
that you should never have to see: massive paychecks, lab results, divorce papers, etc.

34%

THINGS I MADE
you print out but never bothered to look at

7%

TRIPLICATES
of things I made you print out but never bothered to look at

1%

THE DOCUMENT I NEED
RIGHT NOW RIGHT NOW RIGHT NOW

16%

EXPENSE REPORTS
from 3 months ago that I still haven't signed and now can't find

22%

DUPLICATES
of things I made you print out but never bothered to look at

THE PILE OF PAPERS ON MY DESK
A Breakdown

BOSS
WRANGLING
FOR BEGINNERS

*My Two Most Common
Emotional States and
How to Handle Them*

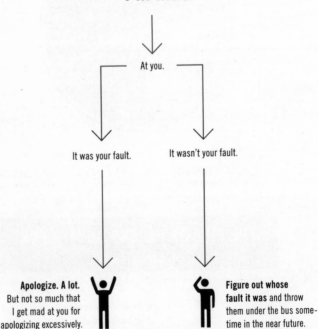

I'm mad

At you.

It was your fault.   It wasn't your fault.

Apologize. A lot.
But not so much that
I get mad at you for
apologizing excessively.

**Figure out whose
fault it was** and throw
them under the bus some-
time in the near future.

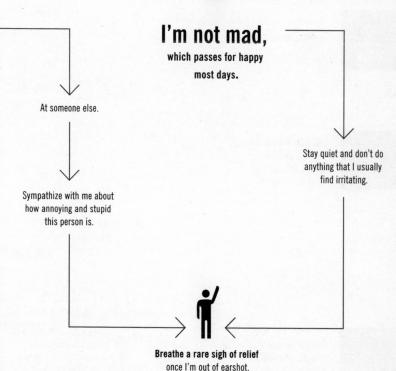

2

I'm not mad,

**which passes for happy
most days.**

At someone else.

Stay quiet and don't do
anything that I usually
find irritating.

Sympathize with me about
how annoying and stupid
this person is.

Breathe a rare sigh of relief
once I'm out of earshot.

IMs FROM HELL: PHONE CALLS

(placing one would be too easy)

BOSS — 3:05 P.M.
Is Bruce in his office?

ASSISTANT — 3:05 P.M.
I'll find out.

BOSS — 3:06 P.M.
well is he??

ASSISTANT — 3:06 P.M.
His assistant is not answering her phone.

BOSS — 3:07 P.M.
just walk down to the 3rd floor and find out. but get someone to cover your phones.

ASSISTANT — 3:08 P.M.
OK I'll be right back. Sheila has the phones covered.

ASSISTANT — 3:12 P.M.
He's not in his office.

BOSS — 3:13 P.M.
Is Mary in her office?

FOOD

The Only Pleasure Allowed at Work,

and Rarely at That

Accusations *(Based on Things That Are My Fault)*

I will not make you work through lunch and then accuse you of having an eating disorder because your stomach keeps making noises that make it sound like you have terrible gas, due to the fact that it's basically eating itself.

Food Orders *(Bizarre)*

I will not give you absurd lunch orders that don't even make sense for someone with food allergies, like "exactly twenty-five half-almonds" or "one-third penne, one-third farfalle, one-third rotini."

Beliefs *(Misguided)*

I will not ask you to sort my M&M's by color, because I believe that the brown and yellow ones contain fewer chemicals.

Taste Tests *(Cruel)*

I will not hand you a cup of liquid, say, "Try this," and then, when you spit it out in disgust, say, "Yeah, I thought the milk smelled sour, but I couldn't tell for sure."

Labels *(Disregarded)*

You will not walk into the kitchen to find me munching on some snacks that clearly have your name written all over them, which I will try to explain by saying, "I thought these were for both of us."

Lies *(Pointless)*

If I tell you I'm a vegan, I'm actually a vegan. I'm not just a rich person putting on a conscientious act, which frequently causes you great difficulties, while secretly eating Big Macs, the many wrappers of which you will discover when you run an errand for me that requires driving my car.

Comfort Food
(Made Uncomfortable)

If you happen to be enjoying some not-particularly-healthy food at your desk during lunch, I won't walk up quietly behind you and startle you by saying, "Fat day, huh?"

Gifts *(Fake)*

When I've ordered too much food and can't finish it, I won't bring my picked-through leftovers out, covered in the weird combination of sauces I like but nobody else does, dump them on your desk, and say, "You can have this if you want." What I'm really saying is "Throw this away for me after enough time has passed so that you don't look ungracious."

Free Food *(Limitations of)*

If it looks like we're going to have a late night, I won't cheerfully say, "Do you want to order some dinner? On me!" (translation: on my expense report for this month, which you will prepare), somehow believing that you'll be happy to have a free meal, no matter what. I'll know that this suggestion is the death knell for your evening, and I'll present it in the appropriately solemn manner while cracking open a bottle of wine for both of us.

Garnishes *(Dramatic Removal of)*

If I receive a garnish on my lunch that I don't care for, even if it has zero impact on the flavor of my food, I will remove it myself instead of calling you into my office and making you remove it awkwardly with a plastic fork and spoon so that you don't touch my food with "your sweaty little hands."

The Lunch Hour
(Awareness of)

When I'm out of the office, ostensibly having lunch with someone as important as I am, I won't call you on your mobile at 1:24 P.M. and say, "Where are you? Why are you on your mobile?!" and then make you roll five calls on your BlackBerry while queuing at the burrito place, your once-monthly semi-junk-food refuge.

Company (Forced)

When we're both having lunch in the office, I won't make you come sit at my desk and eat with me while I browse the Internet and occasionally type work e-mails. You are not a geisha.

Menus (Impermanence of)

I will not blame you when the place I've been ordering lunch from for years changes its menu and you're unable to convince them to keep making the one thing I like from there.

Coffee (Sudden Decisions About)

I will not decide one day that the office coffee, which you've been making for me the same way for the past eighteen months, is disgusting, and make you take an extra thirty minutes out of your day each morning to go to Starbucks, without even offering to get you something there for your troubles.

Kindness (Almost There)

If I offer to buy you lunch, I will ask you what you want. I will not just order you the same (gross) thing I'm getting.

Self-Control (My Lack of)

I will not constantly eat junk food and sweets while giving you reproachful looks, as if there's something you could do to stop me but you're failing at it.

Early Lunches (Really Early)

I will not suggest that you have lunch at 10:45 A.M., because I'm coming into the office at 11:15 after a two-hour appointment with my hairstylist and don't want to "waste all the time" (fifteen minutes) that it takes you to grab some food and eat it at your desk at a normal hour.

Lunch Orders (Specificity of)

I will not tell you to order me "curry" for lunch and then refuse to answer any questions about what country it should be from, what ingredients it should contain, and how spicy it should be.

Projects (Depressing)

I will not suggest that a "fun" thing for you to do would be to pick out a bunch of ready-meals to stock in the fridge, since "we're going to need some quick dinners for all our late nights at the office over the next few months," late nights that you will spend staring hungrily at me while I eat my microwaved food, as it turns out I was using the word *we* in the royal sense, rather than referring to both of "our" needs for food.

Food Odors (Nonexistent)

I will not forbid you to bring any of your "weird homemade food" into the office anymore, "because it stinks up the place," even though what you've been bringing is a series of cold salads and sandwiches, the only things you can afford to eat on your paycheck, and I'm just jealous that you have the ability to assemble your own meals.

Unintentional Insults (Maybe Not So Unintentional)

I will not absentmindedly toss a package of cookies I got in a gift basket onto your desk, saying, "These are for you," only for you to look at the label and discover that they're dog biscuits.

Straws (Paying Attention to)

I will not insist that you put a straw in all of my drinks, and then get mad at you when, distracted by a butterfly outside my office window, I try to take a sip out of the cup and the straw pokes me in the eye.

Authenticity (the Disneyland Version)

After the president of our company goes on at length about how much he loves authentic ethnic food, I will not suddenly decide to be an adventurous eater and ask for your recommendation for a great authentic Mexican restaurant, and then, when you ask how I liked it the next day, sneer and say, "I don't see how 'authentic' a Mexican place that doesn't serve nachos could be," air quotes and all.

Hot Sauce
(Trusting Your Assessment of)

I will take your word for it when you warn me that the hot sauce that came with my lunch is very spicy. I will not scoff at you, insist that "I can take it," and then, five minutes later, come out to your desk to let you know that "we need to order me something else for lunch—I don't really like that [because I disregarded your warning and put hot sauce all over it and now it's inedible]."

Waste *(Painful)*

If I receive a fruit basket as a gift from a colleague, I will not let the basket sit on my desk, untouched, for a full two weeks, while you stare hungrily at the beautiful, expensive pears, apples, oranges, and mangoes, until the fruit is covered in brown spots, and then order you to throw it out, having never offered you or anyone else in the office a single piece.

Forgetfulness *(Stressful)*

I will not tell you at noon that I'll be taking care of my own lunch today and then, at 1:15 P.M., ask you when my salad will be delivered.

Being a Waiter
(for Fifteen Minutes at Lunchtime)

I will not make you lay out my plastic "silverware" on my desk every day for lunch as if you're setting the table for a fancy dinner party, making you rearrange everything if the fork and knife are on the wrong sides or the napkin is not folded correctly.

Routines *(Missing the Point of)*

If I order the same thing for lunch every single day, I will not make you go through the motions of asking me what I want to get for lunch, waiting for me to make a "decision," ordering the food, and then putting up with me complaining when it arrives at 1:15 P.M. instead of 1 P.M. I'll let you just go ahead and order for me so that it arrives at exactly the right time every day, saving both of us time and trouble.

Complaints *(for the Sake of Complaining)*

I will not throw the delicious fresh-baked bread that comes with my favorite salad into the trash every day, but then complain that it's missing when you decide to make my life a little easier and keep it for yourself.

Assumptions *(Dangerous)*

I will not write off your very real food allergies as "convenient" and insist you try something you're truly allergic to, just because whenever I say I'm allergic to something it's because I don't like it or it's not on my current crash-diet plan.

Acronyms *(Purpose of)*

When I want a BLT for lunch, I'll ask you to order me a BLT. I will not, however, spend a solid five minutes describing the contents of the sandwich to you in detail, "just to make sure you get me the right thing."

Bohemianism *(Bourgeois)*

When I tell a colleague that I'm just going to "stay in the office and make my own lunch," I will not actually mean "stay in the office while my assistant spends thirty minutes measuring out all of the strange things I bought at the health food store and assembling them into a 'salad,' the recipe for which was written down by my 'guru' on a patchouli-scented piece of stationery from my sixty-pound-a-session yoga studio."

Misery *(Loves Company)*

I will not decide that a "fun team-building exercise" would be for the entire office to go on a juice cleanse with me, and then, when everyone politely declines, force you to do it, because I don't want to watch you eating lunch outside my office every day while I'm starving myself.

Subterfuge *(Unnecessary)*

I will not regularly order a sandwich that has raw onions on it and then make you disassemble the sandwich, remove the onions, and reassemble it, refusing to just order it without the onions, because "I don't want anyone to think I'm a picky eater."

Coffee Cups *(and Not-So-Subliminal Messages)*

After you buy me a NUMBER 1 BOSS! mug as a gag birthday gift, I will not jokingly ask, "Where's my mug?" every time you bring me coffee in a different cup, so frequently that you soon realize that my "joke" is a real question disguised as such, and I'm actually offended when you don't use my coffee cup to tell me what a great boss I am.

IMs FROM HELL: **EVERYDAY CONVERSATIONS**
(Lunchtime)

12:01 P.M.

ASSISTANT: What would you like to order for lunch today?

12:02 P.M.

BOSS: not sure yet.
I'll let you know.

12:30 P.M.

ASSISTANT: any decision on lunch yet?

12:31 P.M.

BOSS: No.

12:45 P.M.

BOSS: Just get that salad I like.

12:46 P.M.

ASSISTANT: OK. It'll be here by 1:15

12:46 P.M.

BOSS: that late???!!?

12:55 P.M.

BOSS: is it here yet??

12:55 P.M.

Not yet.
Another 15 minutes.

ASSISTANT

12:56 P.M.

BOSS

this is taking too long.

12:57 P.M.

BOSS

you really need to make sure
I make decisions faster.
stay on top of it.

BOSS
WRANGLING
FOR BEGINNERS

*My Meals and My
Mood (a Correlation)*

 **BREAKFAST**

MY FOOD	HOW I FEEL	WHAT TO DO . . .
Cereal and coffee	Normal	Act normally.
Breakfast burrito	Hungover	Walk and talk very quietly, and make sure that all the Diet Cokes in the fridge are ice cold.
Scrambled egg whites	Fat	Compliment me on an article of my clothing.
Black coffee	Mean	Avoid every opportunity for confrontation, which will be next to impossible.

 # LUNCH

MY FOOD	HOW I FEEL	WHAT TO DO . . .
Soup and salad	Normal	Act normally, and quietly celebrate the fact that I've gotten through half a day without descending into a terrible mood.
Fatty sandwich with a side of fries	Still hungover	Bring me another Diet Coke without me having to ask for it, and silently rejoice that there will be no work getting done for the rest of the day.
Fancy chopped salad from a good restaurant, which I offer to buy you something from as well	Indulgent and generous	Thank me profusely, make a note to ask me about that long-overdue pay rise later in the day, and wonder what rare planetary alignment caused me to behave like a real person for once.
Office junk food	Depressed	Smile kindly at me, but not too much, and try not to say much; this mood can quickly turn into anger directed at the nearest person—you.
Super healthy green smoothie	Energetic and productive	Prepare yourself for an afternoon spent catching up on all the projects I've been putting off for the last few months.

44%
DIET COKE

3%
HEALTHY,
NUTRITIOUS,
DELICIOUS
lunch that you
brought from home

10%
OVERPRICED MEAL
from the restaurant in the
building, because you really
needed those fries

16%
FREE
pastries/room-temperature
sandwiches that were left in
the office kitchen

12%
NOTHING,
because I made you
work through lunch for
no reason

15%
JUNK FOOD
aka office heroin

FOOD YOU'LL EAT AT THE OFFICE
A Breakdown

POLITICS AND PARANOIA

How I Actually Spend Most of My Time

Sabotage *(of a Chair)*

I will not make you start an office-wide witch hunt because I am absolutely certain that someone maliciously lowered my chair by half an inch while I was at lunch.

Impressing My Boss
(Results of)

After I encourage you to make a good impression on the president of our company by standing up for your opinions during our weekly staff meeting, you actually do so, and the president responds by agreeing with you and complimenting your intelligence, I will not then become hostile and resentful toward you for the next two months.

Gratitude *(Forced)*

I will not take a half-completed project that you were actually enjoying away from you and give it to my boss's assistant, whom I'm always trying to suck up to, and then spend the rest of the week telling you that "you should be grateful that someone else is doing your job for you."

Promotions *(Received, but Not Really)*

When you do finally get promoted, I will not pretend for the next eight months that you're still my assistant, making you work on all my projects while treating my poor new assistant as if he's capable of nothing more than scheduling and answering the phone.

Other Assistants
(Taking Sides)

When my boss's assistant is being petty and withholding crucial information from you, I will take your side and give you some hints about how to handle him. I will not tell you to "work it out" and then go complain to the other assistant about how childish you're being in an attempt to get on his good side so my meetings get scheduled faster.

Meetings *(Interoffice)*

I will not play chicken with interoffice meetings, always trying to be the last one in, out of some mistaken belief that the last person who goes in to the meeting without actually seeming late looks the most important.

Transitions *(Graceful)*

When you're training my next assistant before you leave, I won't constantly tell you, in your replacement's earshot, to "teach him the right way to do it, not the way you do it," in an attempt to make my new assistant think you're incompetent. I will allow you to do your job well, as you have been doing for the past two years, and give my new assistant the best training possible, making the transition easier for all of us.

Hidden Meanings
(Nonexistent)

I will not obsessively analyze a perfectly innocuous and helpful e-mail you sent me, interrogating you about every turn of phrase and trying to figure out "what you really meant." I will recognize that not everyone is as vague and manipulative as I am.

Social Occasions *(Forced)*

I will not insist that you take my boss's assistant out to drinks at least once a month "to get info" without telling her that I'm forcing you to do so, making you come off as a creepy stalker.

Suggestions *(Too Successful)*

If I've spent the past year you've worked for me telling you to be more like my boss's assistant, I won't fly into a rage when you tell me that you're going to replace him now that he's leaving.

Countersurveillance
(Amateur Hour)

I won't ask you to Google "how to know if you're being bugged" and then expect you to figure out whether or not I am.

E-mail Forwarding *(Sneak Attacks)*

I won't ask IT to set up an alert on my e-mail account that lets me know if my messages are being forwarded without telling you, so that when you forward to another assistant within the company an e-mail I sent you giving my availabilities, I call you into my office and accuse you of "corporate espionage."

Slights and Insults
(Imagined)

If a colleague doesn't answer my e-mail the same day I sent it, I will not call you on your mobile first thing the next morning to ask if you think that colleague is shunning me "because of something I said."

Confusion *(Unlikely)*

If we both come into work wearing the same-color shirt, I will not make you change into the XXL company-branded sweatshirt that's in the storage closet, "because I don't want people to get us confused."

Success *(Paranoia-Causing)*

I will not make you try to sneak into the CEO's office during lunch to delete an e-mail I sent that was incorrect, and then, when you do so successfully, interrogate you about whether you've ever done that to me.

Passwords *(Mine)*

I will not, on a weekly basis, lose the Post-it note on which my e-mail, credit card, online shopping, fantasy football, and/or any other password is written, yet refuse to allow you to maintain a list of all my passwords on your computer, "because it's not secure."

Company Spirit (Versus Sucking Up)

I will not whisper to you during a staff meeting that a colleague of mine is trying to suck up to the president of our company because said colleague reposted a link to a positive news article about the company on Facebook.

Security (Overkill)

I will not insist that you lock my office door every night after I get home, so that the janitorial staff is locked out and you have to DustBuster my floor and empty my trash every morning, due to my overwhelming fear of someone stealing all my "good" ideas.

Taboo (Playing in Real Life)

I will not demand that you find out as much as possible about a certain project that another company is working on but forbid you to ever mention that project by name, so no one will know that I'm looking into it.

Small Talk (Dangers of)

If you find yourself engaging in friendly small talk with one of my colleagues before our staff meeting begins, I will not call you into my office after the meeting and interrogate you about everything he said, and everything you may have revealed about what I'm working on.

Playing a Terrible Game (and Making You My Accomplice)

If one of my colleagues, with whom I'm fiercely competitive, takes a week off work due to an illness, I will not try to start a rumor that said colleague is probably going to quit the business because of it, and insist that you help me by telling all of the other assistants.

Spy Games (Backfiring)

I will not feed you false information in an insane attempt to figure out if you're telling other people things I say to you in confidence, because I've watched way too many spy movies, and then get mad at you when you use that false information in one of the projects I've asked you to work on.

Photographic Memories
(I Do Not Have One)

I will not accuse you of coming into my office and "rummaging through my things" while I was out to lunch, just because my pad of Post-it notes is not where I remember leaving it.

New Communication Technology
(Misinterpretation of)

After I accidentally press the "Video Chat" icon on our IM program while typing to you, causing a video of your face to pop up in a window on my computer, and a video of my face to pop up on yours, I will not make a big show of covering up my computer's built-in web camera with duct tape while giving you the stink eye, as if you were trying to spy on me through my computer.

Recycling *(Blatant)*

I will not use the exact same false compliments on the company's president that you did on me that very morning, without any sense of self-awareness or irony.

Distractions *(Inadvertent)*

I will not accuse you of purposefully trying to distract me on the day of my big presentation when you wear shoes that make more noise than usual on our office's floors.

Brownnosing *(Obvious)*

When I walk into the office first thing in the morning, I will not greet my boss's assistant with a smile and a cheerful "Good morning!" but then, when I reach your desk, snap, "What are you grinning at?" as you hand me my newspapers with a carefully neutral but good-natured expression on your face.

Big Egos (the Wrong Way to Hide Them)

When I achieve a professional success, I will not insist that you send out a company-wide e-mail congratulating me on it, "because if I do it, it'll look like I have a big ego!"

Priorities (Obvious and Depressing)

I will not spend two weeks trying to figure out the perfect gift to give my boss for Christmas, and two hours deciding what to get my spouse and children.

The Seat of Power (Symbolic, Not Real)

If the head of the company is out sick for one of our staff meetings, I will not seat myself at the head of the table and try to run the meeting, as if sitting in a certain chair is enough to give me the power and ability to do so.

Opinions (Having One and Keeping It)

I will not flip-flop my opinion on things to please whoever I'm talking to, cycling through so many different positions that, by the end of the day, you're completely unable to judge what I actually want from you, and therefore can't complete the project I asked you to do, since it's impossible to write something suggesting two mutually exclusive ideas.

Security (Versus Accessibility)

I will not insist on keeping the key to the file cabinets with my personal files in them, which of course I will lose almost immediately, and then, when you reveal that you have a backup key, yell at you for "not keeping my things secure," instead of thanking you for allowing me to get to my passport when I need it.

Secrets *(Unnecessarily Concealed)*

I will not try to cover my computer screen with my hands when you come into my office while I'm looking at my online bank statement, forgetting that you're the person who pays my credit card bill every month, that you set up that online account to begin with, and that you open all my paychecks for me, so I don't get any paper cuts.

OFFICE
INTERACTIONS

A Breakdown by Level

	ASSISTANT	BARELY A BOSS
ASSISTANT	Camaraderie tinged with competition.	Constant bragging about promotion, followed by nagging fear that Assistant is out to get him or her (Assistant is).
BARELY A BOSS	Eye-rolling whenever Barely a Boss asks Assistant to do something, followed by half an hour of grumbling about how Assistant doesn't work for her, followed by a half-assed job on whatever the assignment was.	Fear, distrust, and anger about the fact that someone else got promoted, too; passive-aggressive fake smiles when the other Barely a Boss succeeds; barely disguised vicious glee when the other Barely a Boss fails.
SLIGHTLY SENIOR	A solid belief rooted in experience that Slightly Senior is pretending to be a lot smarter than he or she actually is; begrudgingly does what Slightly Senior tells Assistant to do, since Slightly Senior signs Assistant's time cards.	Fake admiration attempting to hide an agenda to learn as much as possible about Slightly Senior's business and projects, so that Barely a Boss can take them over when Slightly Senior gets canned (with the help of Barely a Boss).
BIG BOSS	Fear, combined with the irresistible urge to make fun of Big Boss's physical appearance, personality, or other quirks with other assistants at every possibly opportunity.	Absolute loyalty, out of the belief that Big Boss handpicked Barely a Boss for promotion; bitterness, once it's discovered that Big Boss barely knows Barely a Boss's name.

ATTITUDE RECEIVER

ATTITUDE GIVER

SLIGHTLY SENIOR

Expects perfection at work from Assistant and also full-time moral support and also a part-time nanny and e-vite designer.

Condescending "helpful" chats that ostensibly give Barely a Boss valuable insight into the industry but are really just a way for Slightly Senior to throw his weight around and prove that he is still in charge of Barely a Boss.

Thinly disguised cutthroat competition; outright hostility, but only behind closed doors. Awkward jokes during Christmas-party speeches about how they might "seem" to hate each other, but really, they're "just like brother and sister."

Fawning admiration in an attempt to get Slightly Senior's own projects pushed through faster than others, with an eye out for any opportunity to push Big Boss off his or her pedestal.

BIG BOSS

Does not care or notice any Assistant except his or her own, and only then when the Assistant is making mistakes.

Remembers Barely a Boss vaguely from when she got promoted; sometimes pays attention when she speaks up at staff meetings, but only rarely.

Tolerates Slightly Senior's incessant brownnosing and attempts to push his own projects ahead of others', because Big Boss knows that Slightly Senior makes it possible for Big Boss to have four-hour workdays.

Either complete trust and partnership, or, more likely, utter distrust and hatred, a relationship that will dictate the entire culture of the company.

BOSS
WRANGLING
FOR BEGINNERS

Requests for Your Opinion
(How to Handle)

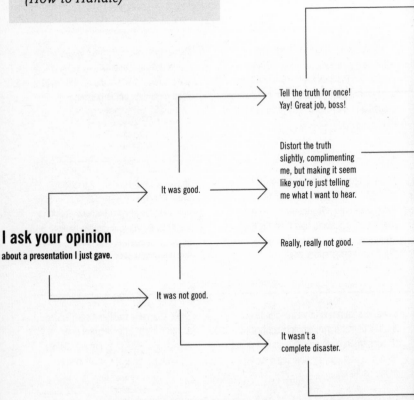

Tell the truth for once!
Yay! Great job, boss!

Distort the truth
slightly, complimenting
me, but making it seem
like you're just telling
me what I want to hear.

It was good.

I ask your opinion
about a presentation I just gave.

Really, really not good.

It was not good.

It wasn't a
complete disaster.

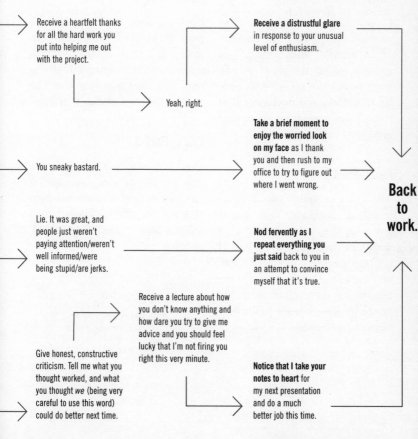

Receive a heartfelt thanks for all the hard work you put into helping me out with the project.

Yeah, right.

Receive a distrustful glare in response to your unusual level of enthusiasm.

You sneaky bastard.

Take a brief moment to enjoy the worried look on my face as I thank you and then rush to my office to try to figure out where I went wrong.

Lie. It was great, and people just weren't paying attention/weren't well informed/were being stupid/are jerks.

Nod fervently as I repeat everything you just said back to you in an attempt to convince myself that it's true.

Receive a lecture about how you don't know anything and how dare you try to give me advice and you should feel lucky that I'm not firing you right this very minute.

Give honest, constructive criticism. Tell me what you thought worked, and what you thought *we* (being very careful to use this word) could do better next time.

Notice that I take your notes to heart for my next presentation and do a much better job this time.

Back to work.

SUPPLIES AND EQUIPMENT

They Will Alternately Save Your Life and Ruin It

Paper *(Time-Saving)*

I will not refuse to buy hole-punched paper "to save the office money" and then yell at you for "going too slow" as you hand-punch the holes of six copies of a 150-page document that I need for a meeting in twenty minutes.

Pens, Part 1

After you've spent two months whining, begging, and pleading with the office manager to stock the pens you love best, I will not decide I like them, too, and dump the entire box into my pen holder, leaving you with only one to get you through to the next office-supply order.

Pens, Part 2

I will not absentmindedly remove pens from your desk, chew on them, and then return them to you without saying anything about the fact that they look like they've been mauled by raccoons.

Pens, Part 3

I will not make you buy the pens you like out of your own pocket "because they're too expensive for the office budget," then shamelessly "borrow" them, permanently.

Pens, Part 4

I will not hoard the office's entire supply of blue and black pens, leaving you only red ink to write with, which I will then complain about, saying it makes me feel like I'm in school again and you're my teacher.

Pickiness

(Counterproductive)

I will not refuse to accept printed documents from you until the folders in the color I like are back in stock in the supply room, and then blame you for causing a delay in our work flow.

Computers *(Jealousy over)*

After I spend six months telling you to get a new computer, and you finally have enough saved to get the latest and greatest, I will not send you a list of links to articles about what's wrong with that computer because I'm jealous.

Chairs *(Torture)*

If my office chair breaks due to my constant fidgeting and swiveling in it, I will ask you to get me a new one as soon as possible. I will not, however, make you switch chairs with me so that you have to deal with the uncomfortable consequences of my actions and then insist that there's just not enough money in the budget right now to replace "your" chair.

Shredders *(Finicky)*

I will not jam the shredder by impatiently trying to shred confidential documents, which I insisted I do myself, even though I already forwarded them to you by e-mail so that you could print them out for me, so you not only have a scanned copy of these "confidential" documents but could print out a hundred more copies of them if you wanted to.

The Thermostat

(Oversensitivity)

I will not be so sensitive to temperature that you have to spend an hour on average every day adjusting the thermostat, because "it's just a little too hot/cold and I can't concentrate."

Plants (Plastic)

I will not insist that you water the fake plants in my office periodically, "for appearance's sake."

Office Supplies (Time-Saving)

I will not insist that every document you hand me be presented in a labeled folder but refuse to buy you a label maker for your desk, so that every time I need something urgently, it takes you an extra ten minutes to hunt down the communal office label maker and switch it back to the font and size I like, while I ask repeatedly, "What's taking so long?!"

Computers (Operating Systems)

I will not make you spend five hours upgrading my work computer, home computer, iPad, and iPhone to the newest operating systems and then, when it's all done, make you spend the next five hours going over every single tiny difference between the old version and the new version with me, because I can't figure out how any of it works.

Technology (Cause and Effect)

If I throw an electronic device, such as a computer mouse, mobile phone, or laptop, against a wall in frustration, and you are kind enough to pick it up and give it back to me, I will not then look at you with all sincerity and ask, "How did this get broken?"

Quality (Pointless)

I will not make you spend a good half hour searching the office for a nice, heavyweight paper on which I can print an important document that I need to sign and send to someone, and then, once I've signed the document printed on that paper, hand it back to you for you to scan, so I can e-mail it.

Postage (Excessive)

I will not insist that I can use the office postage meter myself, "since it's just a letter!" and then later tell Accounting to question you about the £42 stamp that was used that day.

A/V Equipment
(Non-solutions)

My solution to the fact that I can't get the office TV to work will not be to mash all of the buttons on the remote at the same time until the equipment is on settings that the IT department has never even heard of. My solution will be to call you to help me, most likely by just walking me through the very clearly worded, laminated instruction page that is always kept right next to the remote.

IT *(Specificity)*

When there is something wrong with my computer, I will tell you exactly what the problem is and what happened leading up to the error. I will not give you a list of general problems ("it's slow," "something is weird," "my e-mail is weird," "it froze after I did something weird") that makes the IT department hate both of us.

Being a Seamstress *(Not in Your Job Description)*

I will not expect you to keep a sewing kit at your desk so you can sew buttons back onto my shirts—not the shirt that I'm currently wearing, but shirts I bring into the office for you to repair, because I'm a cheapskate and would always rather have you do something for me for free than pay a professional.

Accusations of Waste
(Inflated)

I will not constantly take tissues from the box on your desk, never having my own, and then accuse you of wasting company money "because there's a new box of tissues on your desk every four days!"

Light *(Importance of)*

I will not demand that you keep your small-but-useful desk lamp off for most of the day, in a misguided attempt to jump on our company's energy-efficiency bandwagon, insisting that the dim, flickering fluorescent lights above you "should work just fine."

Power Cords *(Telling Them Apart)*

I will never try to unplug a power cord myself unless I am absolutely sure I have the right one. I won't blame you when I pull the wrong cord out of the wall, cutting power to my desktop and erasing my last hour of work, because I still haven't gotten into the habit of saving things at regular intervals. And, after the third time in two weeks making this mistake, I will not accuse you of "babying me" when you suggest that it might be helpful for you to label each cord clearly with the name of the device it powers.

Scissors *(Yes, I Can Break Those, Too)*

I will not ask to borrow your scissors and return them to you fifteen minutes later, nearly stuck together with tape residue, without even saying thanks.

Buttons *(Excessive Use of)*

When the copier is not working, which is the case about 33 percent of the time, I will immediately come and get you and ask for your help, recognizing that you are depressingly familiar with how to fix it. I will not, however, stand over the machine, repeatedly pressing the big green button until I give up and then come ask for your help, so that when you do fix it, the machine spits out fifty copies instead of just one, thereby giving me the opportunity to give you a lecture about wasting office supplies while you dump almost everything into the recycling bin.

Asking for Help *(It's a Trap)*

I will not spill drawing pins all over my floor and then call you into my office to "help me with something" without first warning you that "something" is the drawing pins that are now stuck to the bottoms of your thin-soled shoes.

Cleaning Supplies *(Ruining)*

I will not manage to get food on my computer screen on an almost daily basis and then ask to borrow your "magic cleaning cloth," which you bought for your own personal laptop and should never have let me know existed in the first place.

Markers *(Mistaken Identity)*

After learning that dry-erase markers can be used to write safely on computer screens, I will not excitedly come over to your desk to see if it works on your desktop, realizing too late that what's in my hand is not actually a dry-erase marker but a permanent one.

Hoarding *(Unnecessary)*

I will not redesign my business cards every month but refuse to allow you to recycle the old ones, "just in case I decide I like them again" (I won't), leaving you with a full drawer of boxes of my business cards and nowhere to store the supplies you actually use every day.

Budgets *(Unbalanced)*

I will not send you out to buy £400 worth of fancy back-to-school supplies for my child but refuse to order a new scanner for the office because "It's too expensive," forcing you to use the one that we have, which takes five full minutes to scan one side of one page and does such a terrible job that I complain about it every time.

Tape *(Difficulties with)*

I will not make fun of you when it takes you more than ten seconds to find the end of a roll of clear tape. (The reason you're trying to find the end is that when I tried to do it myself I ended up throwing it at the wall in frustration and knocking down a framed picture.)

Mechanical Malfunctions *(Inevitable)*

I will not, under any circumstances, try to use any feature on the copier other than the basic "copy" function, since every time that I do, you have to spend thirty minutes pulling out every single door and moving part of the machine until you find the single scrap of paper that I managed to get stuck in its deepest, darkest, hardest-to-reach recesses.

Postage *(Hidden Meanings of)*

I will not make you calculate the exact postage of a package in stamps instead of just running it through our office's franking machine, because I'm sending it to someone I want to impress, and "stamps feel more personal."

BOSS
WRANGLING
FOR BEGINNERS

*My Computer
(Diagnosis and Treatment)*

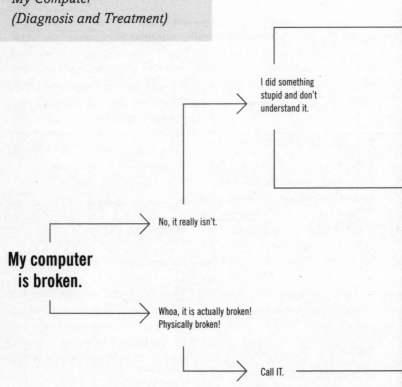

I did something
stupid and don't
understand it.

No, it really isn't.

**My computer
is broken.**

Whoa, it is actually broken!
Physically broken!

Call IT.

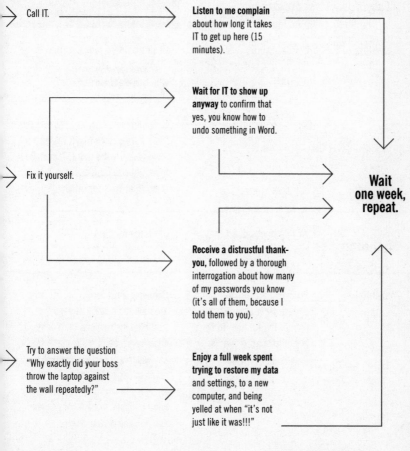

Call IT. ⟶ **Listen to me complain** about how long it takes IT to get up here (15 minutes).

Wait for IT to show up anyway to confirm that yes, you know how to undo something in Word.

Fix it yourself.

Wait one week, repeat.

Receive a distrustful thank-you, followed by a thorough interrogation about how many of my passwords you know (it's all of them, because I told them to you).

Try to answer the question "Why exactly did your boss throw the laptop against the wall repeatedly?"

Enjoy a full week spent trying to restore my data and settings, to a new computer, and being yelled at when "it's not just like it was!!!"

EXPECTATION VS. REALITY

Use of Office Supplies

SUPPLIES	EXPECTED USE	REAL USE
Highlighter	Coloring words yellow so that they stand out from the rest.	Coloring words yellow so that they stand out from the rest, none of which will actually be read.
Pen	Writing things down.	Scribbling furiously as boss dictates a full paragraph without taking a single breath, if a pen can even be found, due to boss casually stealing them from your desk daily.
Pencil	Writing things down that you can later erase.	Chew toy for boss.
Post-it Note	Providing a place to write a clear and concise note or instruction, to be left in a location that is immediately obvious.	Providing a place to try to fit a paragraph's worth of vague, scribbled instructions that, once deciphered, don't really make sense anyway, if you can even find the notes to begin with, since I have a tendency to stick them wherever my hand happens to be resting when I've finished writing them.

SUPPLIES	EXPECTED USE	REAL USE
Paper Clip	Fastening two or more pieces of paper together temporarily.	Automatically linking itself with others of its kind to form an inextricable knot exactly when a single clip is needed most.
Stapler	Fastening two or more pieces of paper together permanently.	Bending staples in every shape possible, except for that of a properly closed staple.
Packing Tape	Sealing up packages for shipping.	Sticking to itself.
Staple Remover	Removing staples from paper without tearing it.	Ripping holes in the upper left corners of paper and then stabbing your fingers.
Letter Opener	Opening letters without having to rip them open inch by inch like a child.	Prop for dramatic fantasies of homicide behind boss's back.
Space Heater	Warming your feet when the office's temperatures dip near freezing levels during summer.	"Accidentally" blowing the same fuse that powers your computer, so that you can't work for the next 30 minutes while maintenance fixes it.

IMs FROM HELL: COMMON CONVERSATIONS
(Monthly)

2:37 P.M.

BOSS

I need to borrow your mobile phone charger.

2:38 P.M.

I think you already borrowed it this morning.

ASSISTANT

2:39 P.M.

BOSS

oh . . .

3:00 P.M.

BOSS

let's order me a new phone charger.

IMs FROM HELL: **COMMON CONVERSATIONS**
(Weekly)

BOSS

11:32 A.M.

Where's my tape?

11:32 A.M.

On the right side of
your desk, next to
your computer.

ASSISTANT

11:33 A.M.

BOSS

I don't see it.

11:33 A.M.

Your other right.

ASSISTANT

11:34 A.M.

BOSS

Found it. Don't make
fun of me like that.

IMs FROM HELL: **COMMON CONVERSATIONS**
(Daily)

5:41 P.M.

Pls come refill my stapler.

5:41 P.M.

I have the staples in here

5:41.P.M.

I just need you to open
it and put them in and
then close it again.

5:42 P.M.

Be right there.

2 TIME

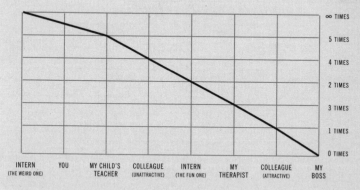

NUMBER OF TIMES MEETING WILL BE RESCHEDULED

∞ TIMES

5 TIMES

4 TIMES

2 TIMES

3 TIMES

1 TIMES

0 TIMES

INTERN
(THE WEIRD ONE)

YOU

MY CHILD'S
TEACHER

COLLEAGUE
(UNATTRACTIVE)

INTERN
(THE FUN ONE)

MY
THERAPIST

COLLEAGUE
(ATTRACTIVE)

MY
BOSS

IMPORTANCE OF PERSON, FROM LOWEST TO HIGHEST

SCHEDULING

In Which You Try to Fit Five Things
Where Only One Can Go

35%
BROWSING THE INTERNET
for "research"

15%
ACCIDENTALLY FALLING
into a long daydream after seeing a
picture of my dream house on
an estate agent's website

15%
**MAKING A CUP
OF COFFEE**
myself for once, justifying
the time it takes by
deciding I need caffeine
to really be able to focus

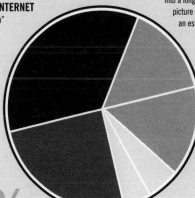

25%
PSYCHING MYSELF UP
to work on the project by reviewing my
colleagues' past failures

5%
**ACTUALLY
WORKING**
on the project

5%
**STOPPING
BY YOUR DESK**
in the hopes that you'll remind
me of something else I need to
do that requires less work

THE TIME I SPEND "WORKING" ON A PROJECT
A Breakdown

Independence *(Good or Bad?)*

I will not get mad at you for "taking the liberty" of pushing a conference call by thirty minutes when I'm running late to the office and not answering your phone calls or e-mails, then, a week later, tell you that you need to "take initiative and act independently, or you'll never get anywhere in this industry."

Disappearing Acts *(Effects of)*

I will not disappear from my office for forty-five minutes to an unknown location, leaving both of my phones on my desk, and then yell at you when I return because you couldn't find me, and now I'm five minutes late for a conference call.

Bad Manners *(Forced)*

I will not make you push a meeting six times, by ten-minute increments, to accommodate the changing schedule of my very expensive hairdresser, and then later berate you for handling the whole thing "in a way that made me look rude."

Vicious Cycles *(Self-Perpetuated)*

When you finally get me to agree to schedule a list of important meetings that I've been putting off for a while, I will not tell you to set them all during a single week in the distant future, and then, when that week arrives, yell at you for "filling my schedule with waste-of-time meetings." And I will not have you then reschedule all the meetings for yet another week in the distant future, infuriating the assistants of the people I was supposed to meet with, who went through their own versions of this situation to get the meeting scheduled on their ends, and causing us to go through this whole process again a few months later.

Scheduled Meetings *(Actually Wanting Them to Happen)*

When I ask you to set up a meeting or conference call, you may assume that I genuinely wish to speak with the people involved, and that I won't say, thirty minutes prior to the scheduled time, "Did I ask you to set this? Make it go away."

Helping Myself (by Helping You)

When you ask me the best way to schedule a big meeting, I will not reply, "I don't know. I don't schedule anymore," and then walk away, leaving you to schedule the meeting in the best way you can come up with based on your own experience, which I later tell you was "unprofessional" and "reflected poorly on me and the work that I do."

Invitations (Actually Reading)

When I receive an invitation to a charity event, I will open it, read it, and then look at my calendar to see if I'm free if the event is something I'm interested in. I will not, however, toss the unopened envelope at you, tell you I want to go to the event, make you reschedule an important dinner with five other people so that I can go to the event, and then, the day before the event, realizing that I misread the return address on the original envelope and that someone I hate is on the board, make you get me out of donating £500 to a worthwhile organization while frantically trying to get the original dinner back on the books.

Mind Reading (Expectations of)

I will not schedule an important lunch myself, not trusting you to be able to get it set up efficiently, forget to tell you about it or put it in my calendar, and then get mad at you when I arrive at the restaurant to find I don't have a reservation.

Out-of-Office Meetings (Why Even Bother?)

I will not tell you to go ahead and set a meeting that will take place at another company, and then, the day before it's supposed to happen, scoff at you when you ask if you can confirm it, asking if "you really believe I'd actually drive to the other side of town for someone that unimportant."

Cancellations (Time-Wasting)

I will not make you bust your ass on Tuesday to get a meeting with five other people set for Thursday and then make you cancel it the morning of, with the vague explanation that "it's not really that important anymore."

Dates and Times
(Usefulness of)

If I put pressure on you to get a meeting set as quickly as you can, I will take the time to tell you when exactly I'd like it to happen. When you finally get it scheduled, I will not yell at you for it happening too soon, too far out, too early in the day, too late in the day, or too close to lunch.

Prima Donnas *(Totally Being One)*

I will not ask you to schedule a meeting with more than two people, give you a single time on a single day that "works" for me, forcing you to beg all the assistants of the other people in the meeting to make their bosses' schedules work around me, and then, after they have done so, realize that I actually have a doctor's appointment at that time, which I never put in my calendar, and refuse to reschedule it, even though there's an appointment available the next day.

Time Zones *(Importance of)*

When on a business trip in a different time zone, I will not leave that time zone and travel to a different one without telling you, and then yell at you when I spend ten minutes listening to the conference call dial-in's terrible hold music (which I force you to do almost weekly, since I'm pathologically incapable of being on time for a conference call) before realizing that you put the call in my calendar at the correct time for the time zone you thought I was in.

Warnings *(Unheeded)*

I will not blame you when other people cancel on a meeting I asked you to set on a Friday afternoon before a three-day weekend, which you already told me they would probably do.

Torture (Just Another Part of Your Job)

I will not make it so difficult and painful for you to go over my upcoming schedule with me that you resort to doing it via e-mail, which causes me to accuse you of being "passive and afraid of confrontations."

Cancellations (Unexpected)

I will not reschedule my Monday-morning doctor's appointment without telling you or changing it in the calendar, and then get mad at you for showing up to work at 9:15 A.M. instead of 9, because you thought I was going to be at the doctor's until 11 A.M.

Impressive Scheduling Feats (Disregarding)

I will not expect you to be able to schedule a conference call with six people who are as busy as I am with only fifteen minutes' notice, and then, if you do actually manage to do so, decide to have you push it to the next day at the last minute, because I suddenly don't feel like having the call today after all.

My Calendar (the Point of Maintaining)

If I insist you spend large chunks of your day updating my calendar with all the details of various meetings you've set for me, including notes on where they're taking place, who will be attending, and what the subject of the meeting is, I will actually look at that information in my calendar, which is easily viewable on my work desktop, my personal laptop, and my smartphone, to be prepared for the next day. I will not rely on you to communicate it to me over the phone every morning and in person throughout the day, because I can't remember things for more than a few hours.

Reminders (Consistency)

When I have a conference call on Monday that starts at 10 A.M., and you remind me at 9:55 that it's starting in five minutes, I will not groan and say, "I know. I have a clock!" but then, when you take my words as an indication that you shouldn't annoy me about the conference call on Friday at 10 A.M., come running out of my office at 9:58 that day, yelling, "We have a call in two minutes! Why didn't you remind me?" and take up five minutes of the call to blame you loudly and excessively for my lack of preparedness.

Scheduling Things Myself
(Dirty Tricks)

If I think it's taking you too long to set up a meeting with someone, I will not call that person's office, schedule it myself, and then send you an e-mail bragging about how I "managed" to set it for a time that I had previously told you would not work for me, because of a "personal appointment" (which we both know is a bikini wax) that I would not move when you asked me to but was more than happy to move for the purpose of making you feel bad at your job.

My Schedule *(Why It's You Who Keeps Track of It)*

I will not forget what day of the week it is, insist that the conference call in the calendar for tomorrow is supposed to be happening today, refuse to believe the e-mail chain you forwarded me to prove that you're right and I'm wrong, and make you call the offices of everyone who's participating to confirm that this is not the case, forcing you to behave like a space cadet in front of several people who previously believed you to be fairly competent.

Meetings *(How Long They Take)*

When you tell me you're pretty sure that I should allocate at least an hour and fifteen minutes for a certain meeting, I will trust you, rather than insisting that it "won't take more than thirty minutes," making you schedule another important meeting starting exactly one hour after the first one begins, and then getting mad at you when the first meeting takes an hour and a half, and I look like a jerk for making the second meeting's participants wait on the uncomfortable chairs in our reception area for a full thirty minutes.

Dinner *(Normal Time of)*

I will not make you schedule all of my work dinners for 8:30 P.M. in order to accommodate the insanely intense yet clearly ineffective exercise class I take, so that you have to wait around the office until 8:45 (the time at which I actually arrive at these dinners) three or four nights a week. I will instead have you schedule them at 7:30 P.M., which will allow you to leave work at a more normal time and has the added benefit of putting the people I'm having dinner with in a better mood by not allowing their blood sugar to dip so low before our late meal.

Light Schedules *(Fault)*

When people I think are unimportant ask me to meet with them, I will not make you schedule those meetings two months out, and then complain to you that "you're not booking my schedule tight enough—I should be way busier than I am right now."

Scheduling Meetings
(the Real Point of)

I will not insist that you schedule a meeting for a day on which I will definitely be out of town, just for the sake of getting the meeting set for as soon as possible to placate the people asking about it, rather than setting it for ten days later, when I can actually attend, and thereby saving you from looking like a terrible assistant when you have to cancel on my behalf and place all the blame on yourself, which I insisted you do.

Your Best Efforts
(Canceling Them Out)

I will get my hair cut and/or styled on weekends, instead of making impulse appointments during the week that make me unable to attend meetings that took you four full days, and several free drinks promised to three different assistants, to schedule.

Power Plays *(Stupid)*

When I finally agree to take a meeting with someone I consider to be far less important than I am, I will not refuse to schedule it for any of the available times that person provides to you and instead insist on bizarre times like 9:07 A.M., 1:21 P.M., or 6:41 P.M., in an attempt to prove that I'm the more powerful person, but really only proving that I'm more insane.

Conference Calls
(Financially Harmful)

I will not make you set conference calls at exactly 9 A.M., so that you have to get to work fifteen minutes before the official start of the workday, for which you will not be paid, due to our company's strict overtime policy, of which I am well aware but constantly justify disregarding, using the excuse that you're "paying your dues."

IMs FROM HELL: **SCHEDULING PRIORITIES**
(Confusing)

10:01 A.M.

what's happening with that meeting I asked you to set with John??

10:01 A.M.

I e-mailed you his available times earlier this morning— those are the only ones that work for him in the next few weeks. I'll resend it.

10:05 A.M.

all of those times are during my trainer.

10:05 A.M.

Would it be possible to reschedule one of your training sessions to fit this in? I can call the gym and send you a list of other times your trainer can do.

10:06 A.M.

no. get other times from them and get this set ASAP. top priority!!!

27%

PEOPLE WHO HAVE BEEN TRYING TO MEET WITH ME for six months, whom I keep putting off because I think they are below me

10%

PEOPLE WHO ARE ACTUALLY BELOW ME, but who are also attractive/related to someone important

10%

PEOPLE I MISTAKENLY BELIEVE I'M EQUAL TO, professionally, who will tell their assistants to put off scheduling this meeting for so long that I yell at you about it

10%

COLLEAGUES WITHIN THE OFFICE, because we're supposed to be working together on a project, even though we hate each other

14%

PEOPLE MY BOSS is forcing me to meet with because he or she does not want to

19%

PEOPLE I'M WORKING WITH on specific projects

10%

PEOPLE GENERALLY RELATED to my business

MEETINGS I TELL YOU TO SCHEDULE
A Breakdown

22%

**PEOPLE WHO ARE
ACTUALLY BELOW ME,**
but who are also attractive/related
to someone important

1%

**PEOPLE WHO HAVE BEEN
TRYING TO MEET WITH ME**
for six months, whom I keep
putting off because I think
they are below me

35%

PEOPLE MY BOSS
is forcing me to meet with
because he or she does
not want to

6%

**COLLEAGUES
WITHIN THE OFFICE,**
because we're supposed to be
working together on a project,
even though we hate each other

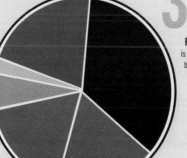

18%

PEOPLE I'M WORKING WITH
on specific projects

18%

PEOPLE GENERALLY RELATED
to my business

MEETINGS I ACTUALLY TAKE
A Breakdown

EXPECTATION VS. REALITY

*My Schedule
and Your Schedule*

	WHAT MY CALENDAR SAYS I'M DOING	**WHAT I'M ACTUALLY DOING**	**WHAT YOU'RE DOING**
9:30 A.M.	Staff meeting	Rummaging through my papers for 15 minutes to find the notes for the staff meeting that you placed on my desk at 8:30 A.M., which I then covered with newspapers and my breakfast.	Insisting that you put the papers I needed for the staff meeting on my desk; reprinting them just in time for me to find the original copies and shoot you a look that says, "I don't even know why I hired you."
10:30 A.M.	(nothing)	Roaming around the office, talking to my colleagues in an attempt to find out if their projects are going better than mine.	Desperately trying to figure out where I wandered off to, because the one person I need to speak to today has, of course, chosen this time of the day to call.

WHAT MY CALENDAR SAYS I'M DOING	WHAT I'M ACTUALLY DOING	WHAT YOU'RE DOING
11:30 A.M. Meeting with [unimportant person with whom I was forced to meet by my boss]	Putting off the meeting by making calls to slightly more important people for 20 minutes, and then, after telling you to bring the person into my office, spending 10 minutes talking to him/her before I text you under my desk to tell you to interrupt me with a fake important phone call.	Trying not to feel guilty every time you have to go out to the reception area and tell the person I'm supposed to be meeting with that, no, I am still "tied up on a really important call"; taking a bathroom break as soon as you're able to finally show the person into my office, knowing that I won't be in the meeting long.
1:00 P.M. Lunch with [old friend who is also in the business]	Racking up a massive bill at an expensive-but-bland chain sushi restaurant, which I will expense, while talking trash about everyone we work with.	Eating food you brought from home at your desk, because you can't afford to eat out, and there's nowhere else in our offices to sit and eat, because our company doesn't really care about its employees.
2:30 P.M. Weekly departmental meeting	Driving like a maniac back from my long lunch, insisting that you go into the conference room and tell everyone that I'm on my way back from a doctor's appointment, even though I do this almost every week.	Trying to ignore the look in my colleagues' eyes as you give them my lame excuse with as much sincerity as possible, because you know that your job at the company depends on my still having one.

	WHAT MY CALENDAR SAYS I'M DOING	WHAT I'M ACTUALLY DOING	WHAT YOU'RE DOING
3:30 P.M.	(nothing)	Actually getting some work done.	Getting twice as much work done as I am, because you have an attention span.
4:30 P.M.	(nothing)	Having spent a full hour working, it's time for me to roam around the office again and see what my colleagues (competitors) are up to.	Desperately trying to figure out where I wandered off to, because the one person I need to speak to today has, of course, chosen this time of the day to call me back after missing me this morning.
5:30 P.M.	Conference call about [project]	Barely paying attention to the call; paying attention instead to a series of videos of people falling over.	Taking detailed notes on the conference call, because you know that I'm not paying attention.
6:30 P.M.	(nothing)	Finally returning the calls of the people who called me today, to find that most of them have gone home, like normal people.	Listening to me complain about how "no one in this town works anymore"; trying to resist the urge to tell me that they actually do, but are just twice as efficient as I am.

WHAT MY CALENDAR SAYS I'M DOING	WHAT I'M ACTUALLY DOING	WHAT YOU'RE DOING
7:00 P.M. (nothing)	Browsing the Internet, waiting, in case someone important calls (they won't).	Trying to finish up some work today so you don't have to do it tomorrow, a concept I have not yet managed to grasp despite all my years in this job.
7:30 P.M. (nothing)	Packing up my stuff to finally leave the office, which will take approximately half an hour, as I'm easily distracted.	Helping me find all the papers I need to take home with me; trying to rush me out the door without being obvious about it.
8:00 P.M. (nothing)	Leaving the office, which you are not allowed to do for another half hour, again in case someone important calls, which, again, will not happen.	Thinking about what kind of beer to pick up on the way home; deciding to go for the kind with the highest alcohol content.
10:00 P.M. (living my life, presumably)	Finally in the mood to work, e-mailing you a series of questions and important tasks that need to get done during the rest of the week, then asking you if you received my e-mails when I don't get a response from you in less than five minutes.	Typing the letters *O* and *K* in response to each of my emails with one hand while the other is holding your fourth beer of the evening; watching dreadful reality TV in an attempt to forget that tomorrow is going to be just the same as today was, but maybe worse.

PATIENCE

Well, Usually Impatience

Rolling Calls *(Actually Giving You Enough Time to)*

When I ask you to get me someone on the phone, I will recognize that you need time to physically dial the numbers. I will not two seconds later ask, "What are you doing?" Similarly, I will not ask you to get me someone and, when you put that person through, yell, "Who is this?" three times before giving you a chance to answer.

Questions *(Answering Rather Than Steamrolling)*

When you ask me a question to clarify something I've told you to do, I will not immediately announce, "I'll just do it myself." I will give you a chance to figure things out for yourself and actually learn something at work for once.

Hurry Up *(So I Can Wait)*

I will not tell you that I need a book "right now," refuse to let you instantaneously download it on my iPad, and instead make you spend two hours calling every single bookstore within a twenty-mile radius, and then, when you finally succeed and triumphantly place the book on my desk, leave it sitting there, untouched, for the next three weeks.

Booking Travel
(Unnecessary Torture)

I will not tell you to book me some plane tickets over the phone because "I don't trust the Internet," wait while you sit on hold, listening to what seems to be a hellish mix of a Sousa march and smooth jazz for forty-five minutes, and then, just when you get someone on the phone, tell you that "I just had my travel agent book the tickets, since it was taking you so long."

Incoming Calls *(Thwarting)*

When you're on the other line and take more than two seconds to answer the ringing phone, I will not yell, "Are you going to get that?" loudly and repeatedly, causing you to get so flustered that you allow the call to go to voice mail while accidentally hanging up on the person you were originally talking to. If I'm that scared of missing a call, I'll answer the phone myself, even if I worry that doing so will make

me seem like I'm not important enough to have an assistant.

Panic *(Contagious)*

When I need you to do something urgent for me, I'll calmly ask you to please stop what you're doing and help me. I will not stomp up to your desk with wild eyes and shout, "Drop what you're doing! Drop what you're doing! Stop right now!" expecting you to throw down the papers in your hands and freak out with me for five full minutes before I tell you what it is I need you to do.

Questions *(Giving You a Chance to Answer)*

When the phone rings, and you answer it, as you do almost a hundred times a day, I will not suddenly appear behind you, bouncing on my toes, whispering, "Who is it? Who is it? Who is it?"

Simple Solutions *(Refused)*

If I need something simple done to my computer, I will not insist that you call IT instead of doing it yourself, "so you don't screw anything up," then complain to you about how long it's taking IT to arrive and wonder if "there's anything you can do to make this happen faster."

Physics *(Battery Charging)*

I will not ask you why my iPad is taking "such a long time" to charge, as if you have anything to do with it or will be able to give me some kind of helpful and accurate answer.

Physics *(Tea Making)*

I will not call you on your mobile phone while you're in the office kitchen to ask why it's taking so long for you to boil water for my tea.

Interruptions
(Counterproductive)

When you're working on something for me, and I've already told you that it's time-sensitive, I will not pace around your desk, looking over your shoulder and periodically asking, "Are you done yet?" I am not a child on a road trip. When you're finished, you will tell me, and if the project is so urgent, surely I have better things to be doing myself.

Computers *(Efficiency of)*

I will not tell you to print out a one-hundred-page document and then yell at you because it's taking too long and I "need to read it right away!" when I could easily double-click on the pdf and have it open on my computer immediately, if I need it that badly.

Rolling Calls *(Unnecessarily)*

When you're away from your desk, doing something I asked you to do, I will not call you on your mobile phone from my office line to ask you to connect me to the person just down the hall. I will dial the four-digit extension myself or just get up and walk down there like any normal non-megalomaniac would do.

Instantaneous Food Delivery
(Impossibility of)

When you tell me that the wait for delivery at my favorite lunch place is forty-five minutes to an hour, I will let you know if I think that's too long and want to order from somewhere else so I can get my food immediately, rather than spending those forty-five minutes to an hour walking out of my office to your desk every ten minutes to ask, "What's taking so long?" causing you to experience your own personal version of *Groundhog Day*.

My Time *(Insulting Allocations of)*

I will not give an intern a full fifteen minutes of my time during the busiest part of the day to discuss his or her professional goals and ask my advice on how the intern can accomplish them, and then, when you ask me during an hour of downtime if I have a moment to discuss your future at our company, give you five minutes before insisting that "I have to get back to work" and that "we'll pick this conversation up later next week" (which we won't).

ASAP *(Does Not Appear on Clocks)*

When you ask me what time I need you to turn in a project, I will not say only the words "As soon as possible," refuse to give you a precise time, and then yell at you when you turn it in because "it's late!"

Socializing *(Usefulness of)*

When you're on the phone with an assistant from another company, making friends in an attempt to gather some information I asked you to get, I will not walk around behind your desk and say, so loudly that the person on the phone hears it, "What's taking so long? I need to know about [info] by the end of the day! Stop socializing!" forcing you to ask the assistant outright for the info, which of course he or she will not give you.

Time Travel *(Impossibility of)*

When I give you a recording of a two-hour conference call to transcribe, I will not expect you to have it finished in one hour and become angry when you don't.

Answers *(Patience Is Relative)*

I will not take a full two hours to respond to a simple yes-or-no question from you but then become irritated when it takes you longer than five minutes to get me the answer to an extremely complicated scheduling question.

E-mail (Faster Than Snail Mail, Slower Than Instantaneous)

After I forward you an e-mail with a large file attached to it, I will not immediately run out to your desk to hover over you and repeatedly ask, "What's taking so long?" until it shows up on your computer, as if this is the first time I've ever sent an e-mail to anyone.

To-Do Lists (Impossible Expectations)

I will not give you a list of fifteen things to accomplish throughout the workday, none of which are easy or simple tasks, and then, thirty minutes later, return to your desk and ask how many things you "still have left to do."

Impulse Buys (Annoying)

I will not make you spend two hours calling every single video store in the city and its surrounding suburbs, looking for an obscure DVD about an artist whom someone I think is important mentioned to me over the weekend, which you could easily get from Amazon were it not for the fact that I decided I want to watch it that very night or not watch it at all.

Deadlines (Clear Versus Unhelpfully Unclear)

If I need you to get something done by a certain time, I will let you know what the deadline is, rather than hovering over you and clearing my throat repeatedly while you work, until you ask if you need to send someone to pick me up some cold medicine.

Lunchtime (Cutting Yours Short, Embarrassingly)

When I go out for lunch, allowing you to eat with your friends for once, I will not sneak back into the office through a side door, twenty minutes before a normal person would have returned, ambush you from behind while you sit at the lunch table with a group of people, and ask loudly if you have "a digestive problem that makes you take twice as long to eat."

Questions *(Defeating the Purpose of Asking Them by Asking Them)*

I will not ask you why it's taking so long to get someone on the phone and expect an answer, which will make the amount of time it takes for you to get that person on the phone even longer.

The Time It Takes to Do Things
(Inability to Change)

I will not ask you "what's taking so long" for you to microwave my lunch, when you're simply following the instructions on the back of the package and can't make any shortcuts unless you think I'll be okay with a plate of partially frozen Pasta Primavera.

EXPECTATION VS. REALITY

How Long Things Take (reality versus my seriously mistaken ideas about reality)

THE TASK	HOW LONG IT TAKES YOU	HOW LONG I'M WILLING TO WAIT
Get someone on the phone	30 seconds to three minutes	10 seconds
Tell me what my schedule is on a day two weeks from now	15 seconds	0.00001 seconds
Schedule a meeting with six other people from six different companies	Two to five days	Four hours, or as long as it takes me to forget and then remember again that I asked you to set that meeting, whichever is less
Turn my "handwritten" (hand-scribbled) notes into a four-page document that has structure and makes sense	Two hours, if you're really good, and I'm willing to help you with particularly difficult squiggles; four hours if not	30 minutes, and my handwriting is totally legible, so what are you bothering me about???

THE TASK	HOW LONG IT TAKES YOU	HOW LONG I'M WILLING TO WAIT
Type an e-mail that I'm dictating to you and send it	The amount of time it takes me to speak the e-mail out loud, plus an extra five minutes to ensure that it actually makes sense and doesn't contain any obvious lies	The amount of time it takes me to speak the e-mail out loud, minus 30 seconds because you're supposed to be able to read my mind
Print a 100-page document in color	Three hours, because I refuse to invest in a printer that isn't seven years old	Five minutes, and "No, I will not look at it in black and white while we wait for it to print in color."
Figure out what's wrong with my computer (when there's nothing wrong with it, and I'm just confused)	The amount of time it takes me to accurately describe the problem I'm having with it	"Let's just call IT and have them handle it."
Figure out what's wrong with my computer (when there is actually something wrong with it)	One to five minutes before you realize that the problem is not due to human error and suggest we call IT	"What is taking IT so long? Did you tell them it's an emergency???"
Text me back on a weekend	One second to one hour, depending on where you are and what your state of consciousness is	"DID U LOSE UR PHONE? WHERE R U????????"

TIME MANAGEMENT

I'd Always Rather Be Checking Facebook

Than Doing My Job

Punctuality *(Meetings)*

When you have reminded me five times that I "really should get going" for my meeting across town, and I still leave twenty minutes late, I will not call you from the car and yell at you because I am running late.

Regular Work Hours

(Knowledge of)

I will not spend all day out of the office, running various personal "errands" (shopping), not taking or placing any calls at all, and then come back at 6 P.M. "ready to work."

Christmas Cards

(Handwritten)

I will not tell you that "we need to deal with my Christmas cards this week" and then put off all your reminders until I've procrastinated so much that I need you to take two hundred cards home over the weekend to forge in my handwriting, "because it's more personal, and I just don't have the time."

Family Time *(Fake)*

I will not make you meet up with me over the weekend to work on something we could have easily done at the office on Friday but didn't, because I decided to go home early in order to "spend some time with my family" (watch crappy TV and eat junk food before my family returns home from school/work/extracurricular activities).

Procrastination
(Shifting the Blame)

I will not put off an important but tedious task for weeks, despite your constant nagging about it, and then blame you for "letting it slip through the cracks" when called out during a staff meeting for my procrastination.

Social Networking
(Blatant Hypocrisy)

I will not insist that if I ran our company, "anyone caught looking at Facebook would be fired immediately," when I myself spend a significant portion of my time on that very site, and we both know it.

Multitasking
(Forced Mismanagement of)

I will not make you spend most of the day doing "research" on decorations for my child's birthday party, and then, as late afternoon approaches, reveal to you

that I also expect you to finish an important project by the end of the day, which I told you earlier to put on the back burner so you could focus "only on the party."

Whole Numbers and Fractions
(Using Them Correctly)

I will not tell you that you have "the whole day" to finish up a project, only to reveal later that by "the whole day" I meant "the first half of the day because I'm planning to leave right after lunch."

Multitasking *(Utter Failures in)*

I will not be so terrible at managing my own time that you have to feed information to me in single-subject chunks, so that I never get distracted by some easier task I can accomplish right away and use to put off doing anything that seems remotely difficult or tedious.

Immediacy *(Faking)*

When we need to get a project done by a certain time, and you hand me your work for feedback,

I will not promise to "get to it right away" and then retire to my office, where my computer will loudly broadcast the sounds of my IMing with my friends for the next forty-five minutes.

Estimates *(Not Complaints)*

I will not take your statement of fact about how long it takes to do something as a complaint and lecture you about your attitude for a good fifteen minutes, when all you were trying to do was make sure that I was aware of how time needed to be managed on a specific project.

Wasting Time *(Yours and Mine)*

I will not take off four hours in the middle of the day to go shopping and then announce upon my return that "it's going to be a late one—we need to catch up!" as if you were somehow complicit in my time wasting.

Traps *(Disguised as Instructions)*

I will not send you an e-mail containing a link to an eight-minute video and the words "Watch this!" and then accuse you of wasting time when I walk by your desk to find you doing exactly that.

Distractions *(Stupefying, Apparently)*

If we have a project that needs to be finished within the next two hours, which will only happen with some serious and focused input from me, and I insist that I'll work on it during my regular morning news-watching time, you will not come into my office thirty minutes later to find me slack-jawed and glued to the TV, a cold, almost full cup of coffee still in my hand.

My Priorities *(Making Them Obvious)*

I will not spend fifteen minutes berating you about a small mistake you made with my lunch order, but only five minutes looking over a fifteen-page document you worked on for two days, which we will be turning in to my boss.

Nagging or Reminding
(Making Up My Mind)

When you remind me of something I need to get done before the end of the day, I will not snap at you and tell you to "stop nagging me!" I will also not then later get mad at you for not "reminding" me enough, because I kept getting distracted by other things/people/Internet videos throughout the day and now don't have enough time to do a good job.

Standards *(Harsher for You Than for Me)*

I will not spend several hours a day playing with the office dogs, "because they help keep my blood pressure down," but accuse you of wasting valuable time whenever you stop to pat one on the head.

Questions *(Unimportant and Non-urgent, Unlike Other Things)*

While you're rushing to get something done for me by a certain time, I will not call you into my office to ask your opinion on some furniture I'm considering for my house, and then act offended when you try to get back to your desk as soon as possible, saying, "What? Is this too unimportant for you to give it your full attention?" Unfortunately, you cannot answer yes.

Instructions *(Incomplete)*

I will not take the time to write you passive-aggressive notes on Post-its that explain that if you really wanted to be a great assistant, you'd do X, Y, Z, but then not take the time to actually explain to you how to do those things well.

Kindness *(Failed Attempts at)*

I will not insist that you leave early in an extremely rare and misguided effort to be nice, ignoring your protests that you really want to finish up a few things so you don't have to do them over the weekend.

Panic *(Unnecessary)*

I will not tell you that "we need to get this project finished in the next two hours, or we're both going to be fired!" causing you to drop everything and work furiously for the next forty-five minutes, and then, when you hand me your work for review, take three hours to look it over, eventually revealing that it wasn't that time-sensitive after all, and I just wanted you to "show a sense of urgency for once."

Your Hopes (Getting Them Up)

When we've had a long day at the office, and it's approaching 6:30 P.M., I will not sigh and say, "I should get going soon," leading you to believe that you might get to leave work before 7:30 P.M. for once in your life, but then spend an hour gossiping with a colleague, so that I leave at 7:30 and you leave at 8, just as we always do.

Urgency (Alternate Definitions of)

I will not wait until ten minutes before you have to leave for the doctor's appointment you told me about three weeks ago and also made sure was in my calendar to remember that I need your help drafting four very long and very "urgent" e-mails.

Wasting Time (Forcing You to)

I will not insist that you have an intern do a task for me instead of doing it yourself, "because you don't need to waste your time on this," even though it will take you twice as long to tell the intern how to do it than it would for you just to handle it yourself, and at least when you do it yourself, you know that it will be done correctly.

Lunch Hours
(Unnecessary Deprivation of)

I will not insist that you stay at your desk during lunch since I'm going to be "working," only to spend the entire hour watching a movie on my computer and not speaking a single word to you.

Your Opinion

(Asking for Efficiently)

If our desks are kind of far away from each other, I will not constantly ask you to come into my office and "take a look at something," which almost always turns out to be a picture or website that I could have easily e-mailed to you instead, so that you didn't have to get up from your chair, walk to my office, look at it, and then sprint back to your desk to just barely catch the phone when it rings.

BOSS WRANGLING
FOR BEGINNERS

Advanced Stalling Tactics

You'd think that, for ten times your pay, your boss would be ten times as likely to want to get work done quickly and efficiently. You would be wrong.

For many bosses, years of experience in an industry means years of experience spent honing their procrastination abilities, so that they can go a full week without doing any kind of meaningful work, undetected. For these bosses, having an assistant means that they shouldn't have to do anything they don't really want to do, ever.

Here are some of the techniques they'll use to stall when you ask them a question they don't care to answer or gently remind them of something they think they're just too important to have to do:

THE TASK	THE RESPONSE	THE MEANING
Mark up a document with notes so that assistant can finalize it	"Put it in my inbox and I'll get to it by the end of today."	"You'll collect it from my outbox next week with no notes on it, and, when asked if I want to make any changes, I will repeat what I said to you just now."
Answer a question that requires more thought than just a "yes" or "no"	"Let me think about it."	"I'm not going to think about it or answer it ever, so I guess you better try to figure it out yourself."

THE TASK	THE RESPONSE	THE MEANING
Make a phone call to a person I hate speaking to, but really should	"Remind me tomorrow."	"Remind me twice a day for the next ten days, until whatever I had to speak to that person about is no longer relevant to what I'm working on."
Compose a reply to an e-mail that requires a certain amount of thought and effort and might take more than two misspelled sentences	"Type up what you think is a good reply, and I'll just copy and paste."	"Spend the next thirty minutes drafting a thoughtful and well-reasoned response, which I will then put off sending for so long that I eventually have to pretend I never got the original e-mail so I don't look rude."
Decide what I want to eat for lunch	"Ask me again in five minutes."	"Ask me again in five minutes, and then repeat this step ten times, so that it's almost lunchtime by the time I make a decision, and I get mad that my food will not arrive at exactly 1 P.M., even though I only told you what I wanted at 12:50 P.M."
Talk to HR about giving you a long-overdue raise, which I only agreed to do so that you'd stop asking about it	"Let's wait until [some arbitrary and completed unrelated event has passed]—trust me, it'll be much more likely to happen then."	"Let's wait until you're so sick of working for me for so little money that you find another, better job and quit before I have to deal with this situation."

IMS FROM HELL: **MULTITASKING**
(Forced)

11:42 A.M.

BOSS: are you done typing up those notes yet?

11:42 A.M.

Just about. I should be done in 15 minutes.

ASSISTANT

11:43 A.M.

BOSS: k

11:43 A.M.

BOSS: what's the soup at Cafe Organico today?

11:43 A.M.

I'll call and ask— one second.

ASSISTANT

11:44 A.M.

It's vegan tomato basil soup.

ASSISTANT

11:45 A.M.

BOSS: oh

BOSS

11:45 A.M.

are you done with those notes yet?

11:45 A.M.

15 more minutes

ASSISTANT

11:46 A.M.

BOSS

that's what you said last time I asked

11:46 A.M.

Sorry—had to stop for a minute to call the restaurant

ASSISTANT

11:47 A.M.

BOSS

so much for multitasking......

11:51 A.M.

BOSS

what's the soup at Sam's Subs today?

WEEKENDS AND HOLIDAYS

Yeah, Right

To-Do Lists *(Wrong Way to Do)*

I will not send you fifteen e-mails on Sunday night, each containing an individual task I need to accomplish the next week, just because I don't want to forget about them and am too scattered to take the time to compile them into a single e-mail.

The Holiday Spirit *(Opposite of)*

I will not send you an angry e-mail on Christmas Eve—subject line "IM FURIOUS," contents describing the many small ways in which you have failed me over the past month—just because my Internet in my house stopped working for thirty minutes and I wasn't able to respond immediately to the head of my department's casual Happy Holidays e-mail.

Regifting *(Completely Obvious)*

When you give me a nice bottle of wine for my birthday, because my personality is so deficient that you can't come up with anything else that I might enjoy, I won't leave it on my desk for months and then cheerfully give the dusty bottle back to you for Christmas.

Valentine's Day *(Not Taking Care of Things at All)*

If I tell you that "I'll take care of the Valentine's Day reservations myself," I mean that I will make them myself. I do not mean that I will put off taking care of it until 7 P.M. on February 13, and then scream at you when all the hot restaurants in town turn out to be fully booked.

Television Technology
(Handling It Myself)

I won't make you come over to my house on a Saturday morning to help me set up my Sky Plus and make sure that all *Real House-wives* episodes will be recorded in the future, so that you're forced to fumble around with my five remotes while my significant other, my tech-savvy teenaged children, and I stand around and watch, sipping our coffee.

Your Leash *(Otherwise Known as Your Mobile Phone)*

I will not call you on your mobile phone over the weekend and get mad at you when you're not able to get to your computer in five minutes, because you're on the other side of town, enjoying yourself for once.

Checking E-mails
(Normal Frequency of)

If I send you an e-mail over the weekend, I will not call you and/or leave you an angry voice mail if you haven't responded five minutes later.

Three-Day Weekends
(Canceled for Fake Reasons)

I will not generously give you Friday off so you can enjoy a quick holiday with your family, and then rescind the offer on Thursday afternoon "because we're just too busy, and I really need your help," only to have you sit in the office and do nothing for ten hours the next day because I woke up with a slight headache and am now taking the day off myself.

Distant Errands
(Absolutely Ridiculous)

When you're halfway across the country during the holidays, I will not insist that you get a hard copy of a document to one of my colleagues, despite the fact that that colleague has been perfectly happy to receive digital versions in the past. I will not force you to drive twenty miles to the one FedEx center that's open late and spend £50 of your own money on overnight shipping, with the knowledge that I will almost certainly refuse to reimburse you for it, since once of my favorite things to say has always been "I'm not going to pay for your failure to think ahead."

Waiting (Without Anything Good for Yourself at the End)

I will not make you come over to my house on a Saturday at 8 A.M. so I don't have to stay inside my own home for the four-hour window in which the cable guy is expected to arrive.

Emergencies (Not So Much)

I will not leave you a panic-ridden voice mail over the weekend insisting that you return my call immediately because "it's an emergency!"—only for you to call me back to find that I need you to pick up a case of wine for the party I'm hosting in eight hours.

Invitations (Expensive)

I will not ask you to meet me at a restaurant over the weekend so we can work on something we didn't get done during the week, encourage you to order a glass of wine and a snack while we work, and then not offer to pay for it, even though the restaurant I've chosen is only affordable to someone who makes as much as I do, and I've stolen a four-hour chunk from your weekend.

Commuting (Unnecessary)

After you spend an entire week trying unsuccessfully to get me to finish a project, I will not decide that it needs to get done over the weekend and make you meet me in person to do the work that we could easily do over e-mail or the phone, turning a project that would have taken you about forty-five minutes to complete into a three-hour ordeal, two hours of which are spent driving across town and then back again.

Kind Warnings
(Consequences of)

If you are considerate enough to let me know that you have a busy weekend ahead and therefore might not be able to respond to my e-mails or texts immediately, I will not insist that you give me a detailed itinerary of where you will be at what times, "just in case of an emergency," forcing you to come up with a series of made-up events in an attempt to escape from me for a full twenty-four hours, for the sake of your sanity.

Early-Morning Phone Calls
(Completely Unnecessary)

I will not call you at 8 A.M. on a Saturday to ask you to book me a hair appointment for 3 P.M. that same day, when both of us know that my hairdresser's number is in my phone's contacts, listed under the unambiguous name "HAIR."

Glances *(Day-Ruining)*

Upon hearing at an all-staff meeting that our offices will be closed on Friday for the holiday, I will not remark, "Well, I'll still be here,"

and then throw you a friendly look that quickly becomes threateningly insinuating.

Taking Time Off *(Not the Same as Slacking Off)*

If you ask for a reasonable amount of time off, and I give it to you without any kind of hassle, I will not later bring up the time that you took off as an example of how you're slacking on the job when you ask me for a raise.

Convenience *(for Me, Not for You)*

I will not make you go to a theater box office to queue for tickets first thing on a Saturday morning because I didn't want to pay the £15 online booking fee on tickets that will cost me £250.

Impositions
(Sleep-Depriving)

If I ask you what time you think you'll be up on a Saturday morning so I can call you to discuss something, and you answer, "Probably around ten," I will not reply, "How about nine instead?"

Complaints *(Being Able to Give but Not to Receive)*

I will not complain constantly about how much I have to work over the weekends and how it's affecting my personal life, but then accuse you of having a terrible work ethic when you commiserate, even though you work exactly as much as I do, if not more, on Saturdays and Sundays.

Weekend Fun *(Completely Ruining Your Chances for)*

I will not tell you that I need to meet up with you at nine sharp on a Saturday morning, ruining your plans to go out and actually have fun for once on a Friday night, and then, at 8:30 A.M. on Saturday, text you that something's come up (most likely a hangover) and I need to meet you at 9 A.M. sharp on Sunday instead, thereby ruining your Saturday-night plans as well.

My Errands *(Managing to Take from Bad to Worse)*

I will not decide that it's a waste of your time and the company's money to have you run personal errands during regular work hours, and therefore insist that you do all these things for me on the weekends instead, for no pay, "because I can't do everything myself around here!" ("here" being my house, and "myself" being someone who is married with children, can drive, and employs a housekeeper).

Good Intentions *(Bad Execution)*

If I want to wish you Bon Voyage while we're both on holiday, I will send you an e-mail or a friendly text. I will not, however, call you on your mobile phone in the middle of a family dinner, wish you happy holidays, and then manage to shift the topic of conversation to all the things I need you to do once we're back in the office, because I'm not used to speaking to you without giving you some kind of instructions.

Holiday Invitations
(Unwanted)

When I overhear you saying that you'll be staying in town for Christmas, since you don't have enough time off to go visit your family, I will not invite you over to my family's Christmas dinner and then act offended when you politely decline, because you (a) already made plans, (b) know exactly how strained my relationships with my spouse and adolescent kids are, due to the fact that I make you connect me to their mobile phones for personal calls and then stay on the line in case I need you to conference another family member on, and you don't want to be anywhere nearby when we're all forced to sit together at the same table for an hour, and (c) are smart enough to figure out that the only reason I want you there is so you can try to defuse the situation.

Weekend Work
(Unnecessary)

I will not make you work on a project all weekend and then not even look at it until Thursday of the following week, meaning that you could have easily turned the project in to me on Wednesday night instead of Sunday night and enjoyed two days of rest for once.

Terrible Weekends
(Comparisons of)

I will not complain to you about how "disappointing" my weekend at an exclusive spa was, when I know very well that you spent those same two days compiling thirty pages of research on a very boring subject for me.

Surprises (Unpleasant but Not Your Fault)

I will not scream at you when you send out my Christmas cards, which feature a picture of my entire family smiling disingenuously at the camera, in exactly the punctual manner I told you to, which turns out to be exactly twenty-four hours before my spouse ambushes me with divorce papers.

Cooking (Impossibility of Teaching Me How)

After discovering that you enjoy food and are pretty good at cooking, I will not put you in charge of planning the menu and shopping for my family's Christmas dinner, which, despite the fact that you chose the most basic recipes that even a middle schooler could make without much difficulty, I still manage to turn into a blackened mess, pictures of which I will text you throughout the evening, along with implications that it's all your fault, so that you're unable to enjoy the delicious dinner you cooked for your own family.

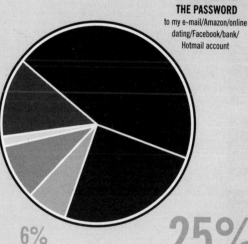

45%

TO ASK YOU FOR
THE PASSWORD
to my e-mail/Amazon/online
dating/Facebook/bank/
Hotmail account

13%

TO ASK FOR A "FAVOR,"
to which you're not allowed to
say no, and which will take up a
sizable chunk of your weekend

1%

TO ASK IF YOU CAN
COME PICK ME UP
from a bar, because I'm too
cheap to get a cab

10%

TO TELL YOU
to remind me to do
something next week,
which I could've easily
e-mailed you about
instead

6%

CONFUSING ARSE
DIALING

25%

TO ASK YOU A QUESTION
you answered five times already
during the previous week

MY CALLS TO YOU OVER THE WEEKEND
A Breakdown

TEXTS FROM HELL: SATURDAY-NIGHT CONVERSATIONS

(Joys of)

7:01 P.M.

BOSS
what's my password for amazn?

7:14 P.M.

BOSS
Amazon

7:32 P.M.

BOSS
Hello?

7:47 P.M.

BOSS
???????

8:04 P.M.

BOSS
Hello?

8:17 P.M.

BOSS
did u lose ur phone?

BOSS 8:34 P.M.

are u ignoring me?

BOSS 8:54 P.M.

HELLOOOOOO?????

BOSS 9:06 P.M.

were going 2 have 2 talk about this on Mon

9:07 P.M.

So sorry! Was in a movie. Phone was off. **ASSISTANT**

9:08 P.M.

Your password is MILF1958 **ASSISTANT**

BOSS 9:32 P.M.

thx

BOSS 9:34 P.M.

ur phone should always be on vibrate

BOSS 9:37 P.M.

what if I needed something from Amazon right away? could have been an emergency.

9:37 P.M.

OK, will do in the future **ASSISTANT**

E-MAIL CHAINS FROM HELL:
The Sunday-Evening Scheduling Special

SUBJECT: JOE MTG
FROM: BOSS
TO: ASSISTANT   8:12 P.M.

Pls make sure tmrrw's mtg is confrmd.

SUBJECT: RE: JOE MTG
FROM: ASSISTANT
TO: BOSS   8:13 P.M.

I confirmed on Friday afternoon. We're all set.

SUBJECT: RE: RE: JOE MTG
FROM: BOSS
TO: ASSISTANT   9:34 P.M.

No. Call his asst. Make sure.

SUBJECT: RE: RE: RE: JOE MTG
FROM: ASSISTANT
TO: BOSS   9:35 P.M.

Unfortunately their offices are closed, and I don't have a
mobile number. I'll email, though.

SUBJECT: RE: RE: RE: RE: JOE MTG
FROM: BOSS
TO: ASSISTANT   9:59 P.M.

WHY NO MOBILE???????

SUBJECT: RE: RE: RE: RE: RE: JOE MTG
FROM: ASSISTANT
TO: BOSS   10:01 P.M.

She just answered my email. The meeting is still confirmed.

SUBJECT: RE: RE: RE: RE: RE: RE: JOE MTG
FROM: BOSS
TO: ASSISTANT   11:58 P.M.

Fine. Next time get mobile tho. Better than email. What if i
had to cancel RIGHT NOW and u couldnt get ahold of her
and she only saw the email 2morrow morning? It would
make me look RUDE.

TEXTS FROM HELL:

Measuring the Alcohol Content of My Drinks by the Content of My Texts

9:30 P.M.

BOSS: did u get my e-mail?

9:31 P.M.

I haven't gotten one from you in the past 8 hours, so no, I don't think I did.

ASSISTANT

10:05 P.M.

BOSS: why not???????

10:06 P.M.

I'm sorry, but I don't know why I didn't get it. Is it in your sent folder?

ASSISTANT

10:35 P.M.

BOSS: what? howe cld i even know that? i dont have m y laptop

10:36 P.M.

Could you please resend it?

ASSISTANT

10:47 P.M.

BOSS: idnt even rmember what it says. thats ur job not mine!!!!!

10:48 P.M.

Would it be better to deal with it when you're back at your computer tomorrow morning?

ASSISTANT

11:03 P.M.

BOSS

NO HAV 2 do it 2night

11:04 P.M.

BOSS

URGT!!111111111

12:37 A.M.

BOSS

pls find me taxi service nmber

12:37 A.M.

No problem.

ASSISTANT

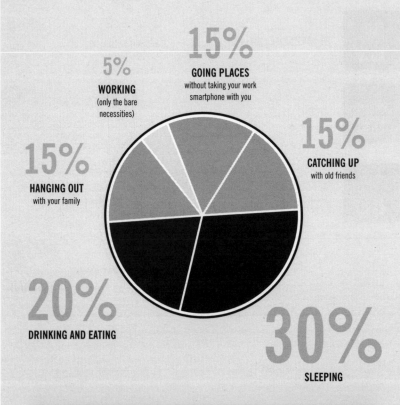

15%
GOING PLACES
without taking your work
smartphone with you

5%
WORKING
(only the bare
necessities)

15%
CATCHING UP
with old friends

15%
HANGING OUT
with your family

20%
DRINKING AND EATING

30%
SLEEPING

HOW YOU'D LIKE TO SPEND YOUR HOLIDAY
A Breakdown

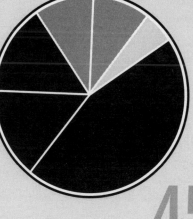

15%

THINKING ABOUT WHAT AN
AMAZING BOSS I AM
and being thankful that
you work for me

10%

TELLING ME WHAT
AN AMAZING BOSS
I AM

10%

SLEEPING WHILE
DREAMING
about how much you
can't wait to get back to
work and help me with all
my needs

5%

CATCHING UP
with old friends,
hanging out with your
family, drinking and
eating

15%

THINKING ABOUT WORK

45%

WORKING

HOW I'D LIKE YOU TO SPEND YOUR HOLIDAY
A Breakdown

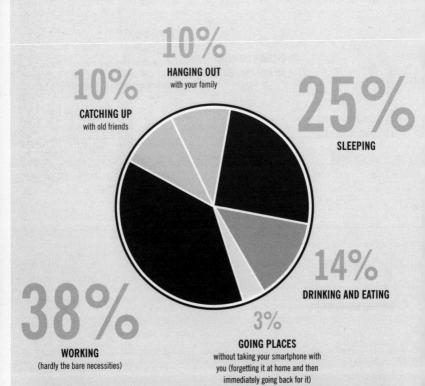

10%
HANGING OUT
with your family

10%
CATCHING UP
with old friends

25%
SLEEPING

14%
DRINKING AND EATING

38%
WORKING
(hardly the bare necessities)

3%
GOING PLACES
without taking your smartphone with
you (forgetting it at home and then
immediately going back for it)

HOW YOU'LL ACTUALLY SPEND YOUR HOLIDAY
A Breakdown

3

COMM
un-
ICATION

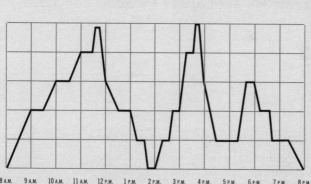

INTENSITY OF COMMUNICATION WITH ME

SCREAMING AT YOU

RAPID-FIRE IMS ASKING FOR INFORMATION ASAP

FACE-TO-FACE TALKING

CONVERSATION HELD OVER PHONE

E-MAILING

RADIO SILENCE

8 A.M. 9 A.M. 10 A.M. 11 A.M. 12 P.M. 1 P.M. 2 P.M. 3 P.M. 4 P.M. 5 P.M. 6 P.M. 7 P.M. 8 P.M.

TIME OF DAY

CLARITY

Technically, We Both Speak the Same Language

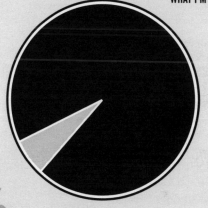

94%
WHAT I'M THINKING

6%
WHAT I'M SAYING

WHAT I WANT YOU TO TYPE WHEN I'M DICTATING TO YOU
A Breakdown

Specificity *(Importance of)*

I will not tell you to "send me that thing from a month ago," "get me that thing I wanted to get," "resend me that document from two weeks ago—you know, the one with the guy," or "find that intern I was talking to last month when you weren't at your desk." I will learn more nouns, verbs, and adjectives and have them readily at my disposal.

My Handwriting *(Being Able to Read It Myself)*

When I give you ten pages of handwritten notes to type up, and you come into my office a few minutes later asking for help deciphering a particular squiggle, I won't stare at it for a minute or so with a look of deep concentration on my face and then hand it back to you, saying, "No idea."

Y/N, Part 1

If you send me an e-mail containing more than one yes-or-no question, I will not reply with just a "Y" or an "N," assuming that you can figure out which question I was answering.

Y/N, Part 2

If you send me an e-mail containing one or more questions that aren't even close to being of the yes-or-no variety, I will not respond with only "Y" or "N," leaving you to psychically decode that one letter to figure out my real answer.

Y/N, Part 3

I will not get mad at you for "sending me too many e-mails," after you've realized that you can only present me with one yes-or-no question per e-mail if you ever want it to get answered in a clear and accurate way.

Answers *(Necessity of)*

I will not vaguely instruct you to do something and then suddenly disappear for forty-five minutes, leaving you with many questions that need to be answered before you can complete the task correctly, and then, when I return, ask, "Why isn't this done already?"

Opposite Day *(Every Day)*

I will not frequently say the exact opposite of what I mean, and then accuse you of condescending to me when you start to double-check regularly to make sure you understand what it is I actually want you to do.

People *(Knowing Which Is Which)*

I will not ask you to send an e-mail to Person A, insist that I do in fact mean Person A when you double-check with me before sending it, and then yell at you after the e-mail is sent, because I actually meant Person B, and you were supposed to know that.

Near-Impossible Tasks *(Appreciation of)*

I will not ask you to find me a book I want to read, the only description of it being that "the cover is blue and red, it's funny, and about a guy who lives with his mother," and then, when you actually do find the one I was talking about, berate you for taking two days to do so.

Accusations *(Unwarranted)*

When you ask me to be more specific about something, I will not accuse you of being lazy and wonder out loud why I have to do all your work for you. Particularly if all you needed to know was whether I wanted a bottle of red wine or white.

Attitudes *(Counterproductive)*

I will not be so prickly about clarifying what I mean that you become fearful of ever asking me to do so, and therefore take twice as long to do your job while you puzzle over my incoherent e-mails and creatively spelled texts.

Deceptions *(Confusing)*

I will not tell you to "hop off the line" during an apparently sensitive phone call, and then later get mad at you because I didn't actually want you to get off the line—I just wanted the other person to think that you were.

Dictionaries (Usefulness of)

I will not decide to add a new word or abbreviation to my vocabulary without knowing what it means, resulting in several weeks of confusion while you work up the courage to ask me if I actually know the definition of my new favorite "slang word," which my misuse of is actually causing me to insult over half of our coworkers on a daily basis, by accident for once.

Different People
(Telling Them Apart)

When there are two people with the same first name in our offices, I will not constantly get them confused, even when you start referring to them as "First Name + Job Title" in an attempt to make both of our lives easier.

Questions (Excessively Punctuated)

I will not send you e-mails that consist of one or two words followed by almost as many question marks as there are letters in those words, causing us to have a lengthy exchange before you can actually figure out what I want you to do. Instead, I'll take the time to compose a complete question that you can answer quickly and decisively.

Time Zones (Difference in)

When I'm in a different time zone, and I ask you to schedule a conference call for me at a certain time, I won't fail to specify which time zone I'm talking about, ignore your e-mails asking me to do so, and then get mad at you when you incorrectly decide that I must mean the time local to where I am, since that would make the most sense.

Answers (Ignored)

When I ask you a question, and you answer with an unqualified "No," I will not assume that you meant "Possibly," just because the answer you gave me isn't the one I wanted.

"Lengthy" E-mails (Not Really That Long at All)

I will not accuse you of being unclear when you send me an

e-mail that is longer than three sentences, just because I'm too lazy to read things that long.

My Children (Telling Them Apart)

I will not get the names of my children confused and then get mad at you when you order an appropriate gift for the one I told you to buy a gift for but not the one I actually meant.

Dietary Terms (Using the Right One)

I will not tell you to order me a "vegan burger" for lunch, using the word *vegan* to mean "vegetarian" without you realizing it, and then come out of my office holding the bun open and yelling, "Where is the cheese on this???"

Nicknames (Consistency in)

After I've fallen into a pattern of referring to one person as "that guy," another person as "that dude," and a third person as "that idiot," so you actually know who I'm talking about when I say those words, I will not suddenly switch up those "nicknames" without any warning, causing several days of confusion as you try to relearn my special language.

Three-Letter Words (Importance of)

I won't accidentally omit the word *not* from an e-mail that was only four words long to begin with, and then yell at you when you do the thing I completely failed to tell you not to do.

Writing Utensils (Knowing the Difference Between)

When I ask for a pencil, I will actually want you to bring me a pencil, instead of accidentally asking you to bring me a wooden cylinder that I will then break in half and throw to the ground while shouting, "No! A pen!"

Questions (Fear of Asking)

I will not roll my eyes and sigh loudly every time you step into my office without me asking you to do so, creating an environment so hostile to question asking that you spend most of your time trying to figure out what I actually mean and fearing the repercussions of misunderstanding me, rather than doing what I want you to do.

Non-answers *(by E-mail)*

When you reply to an e-mail I've sent you asking for clarification, I will not just forward the original e-mail to you again, as if that solves anything.

Questions *(Outdoing You Punctuation-Wise)*

When you send me a very simple yes-or-no question by e-mail, IM, or text, I will not reply with only "??????????????" If I don't understand what you're trying to ask me, I will tell you which part of your question doesn't make sense to me (a problem most likely due to my only reading every other word of what you wrote and then giving up after three sentences).

Pointing *(Usually Applies to a Person)*

I will not point at someone in the office and say, "Set a meeting with her," only to later reveal angrily, once you've e-mailed me times that work for the person you thought I meant, that I actually wanted you to set a meeting with the person whose office was behind the person you thought I was pointing to.

Interns *(Usefulness of Names)*

I will not request the help of "that intern I like," when the person that refers to changes from week to week, depending on said intern's revelations of important parents, shortness of skirts/ tghtness of dress shirts around buff upper arms, or abilities to compliment me in ways that feel sincere.

Meetings *(Meaning, Meeting in Person)*

When I tell you to set a meeting with five people, I will mean for you to set a meeting. I will not act surprised, and angry with you, when they all show up at the office at the time it turns out I actually wanted a conference call to happen.

Easy Answers *(Not So Easy After All)*

When I choose to use the syllables "Uh-huh" for yes and "Uh-uh" for no, I will make sure that there is a clear difference between them, so that you don't have to turn a simple yes-or-no question into a series of two to four questions to finally get a clear answer.

Page Numbers
(Usefulness of)

When I tell you that you need to rewrite "paragraph two" of a document, I will mean the second paragraph of the entire document, not the second paragraph of the page I was thinking of but never actually said out loud.

E-MAIL CHAINS FROM HELL:
Advanced E-mail Translation

Sometimes it will seem like the main part of your boss's job is to confuse you as much as possible when e-mailing you. After a few months, you'll be able to decipher the everyday vagaries of your boss's special style of writing, but don't get too comfortable—all bosses always have more tricks up their sleeves.

Here are some examples of advanced confusion tactics, and their translations into normal, understandable language:

SUBJECT: ????
FROM: BOSS
TO: ASSISTANT

Con plan???

Translation: What's the plan for the convention I just decided to attend, which you were expected to predict, even though yesterday I said I wasn't going???*

---

*Note that effort was put into adding extra question marks but not into the actual content.

Mps pls.

Translation: Please print out a map for every place I might be going in the next week, and then present them to me so I can pick out which one I actually want. Any attempt to ask me which specific location I actually want directions to will be met with a combination glare/shrug.*

----

8 13 14 34 49 52

Translation: This list of numbers may be:

a) Something I'm going to forget, so I'm e-mailing it to you to force you to ask what it is and therefore remind me about it.

b) My selection from a larger list of things that I may forward to you in five seconds, two hours, or never.

*Note that an effort was made to be polite and punctuate correctly, but such consideration was not applied to spelling or specificity.

c) Something I meant to send to someone else. When I realize that I sent it to you, I will tell you to delete it from your computer immediately and ask, "Did you read it?" as if you could derive any meaning whatsoever from doing so.

d) A number for a lottery ticket I bought, because making twelve times the amount you do per year isn't enough for me.

e) Two or more of the above.

IMs FROM HELL: SPECIFICITY
(Delayed)

12:15 P.M.

BOSS

what's the name
of that guy?

12:15 P.M.

Which guy?

ASSISTANT

12:15 P.M.

BOSS

you know, that guy.
the one whos name
i can never remember.

12:16 P.M.

I don't mean to be flippant,
but you're going to have
to be a little more specific.

ASSISTANT

12:16 P.M.

BOSS

hes really annoying

12:16 P.M.

BOSS

i never take his calls

12:17 P.M.

BOSS

hes at that company
i hate dealing with

. . . . . .

he wears a really
obvious toupee

Bob Richards.

thats it

took you long enough

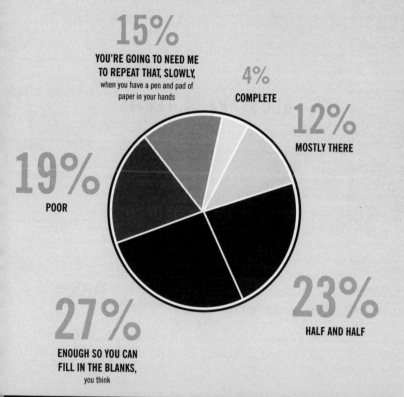

15%
YOU'RE GOING TO NEED ME TO REPEAT THAT, SLOWLY, when you have a pen and pad of paper in your hands

4%
COMPLETE

12%
MOSTLY THERE

19%
POOR

23%
HALF AND HALF

27%
ENOUGH SO YOU CAN FILL IN THE BLANKS, you think

YOUR UNDERSTANDING OF WHAT I SAY TO YOU IS, ON AVERAGE
A Breakdown

THE TELEPHONE

Torture Device Number one

GLOSSARY OF TERMS

The telephone is a large part of any assistant's job. A good assistant can operate a telephone with the same skill and artfulness with which a classical musician plays an instrument. Connecting eight people for an impromptu conference call comes as easily to a good assistant as a Bach concerto comes to Yo-Yo Ma. But no one ever threatens to fire Yo-Yo Ma when he makes a mistake.

There may be some phone vocabulary in this book that you're unfamiliar with, because you haven't ever had to deal with these issues; hopefully, you never will. Following is a guide:

phone sheet *(n)* A list of the boss's incoming and outgoing calls, reminding both boss and assistant who needs to be called back and who needs to be resented for not having called the boss back yet.

Example: Billy's boss doesn't understand that he can see the phone sheet on his own computer, and therefore makes Billy yell the entire list of thirty names out in order every time he wants to make a call, drowning out everyone else's attempts at verbal communication on a regular basis.

rolling calls *(v)* Calling a ton of people back in succession until someone actually picks up. Especially fun when the boss is on his or her mobile phone and the assistant has to use the Conference button on the phone to connect the call and then the Drop button to disconnect it rapidly afterward before the boss starts making mean comments about the person he or she was just talking to.

Example: Peggy Sue's favorite part of her job is rolling calls, because it's time her boss spends yelling at other people instead of just her.

leaving word *(v)* The fancy way of saying you called someone back but that person wasn't there, so you told that person's assistant to put you on the phone sheet. Or you left a mechanical-sounding voice mail that the assistant will later listen to and wish it wasn't so long before you gave the call-back number.

Example: Whenever Bobby tells his boss that he left word for someone, his boss gives him a dirty look, as if Bobby is somehow sabotaging his boss's career, call by call.

dropping calls *(v)* Calling someone after regular work hours to avoid having to actually speak but to still be able to say you called back.

Example: Sally's boss, Jennifer, has a reputation for dropping calls on people she doesn't want to talk to, but no one will call her on it, because she's very important and yells a lot.

conference calls *(n)* A cacophony disguised as a substitute for a meeting, these calls quickly become bloated and unwieldy as more and more people are added, to make sure no one's feelings are hurt by being left out. If you're lucky, your boss will actually get on the call on time. If you're unlucky, your boss will always try to be the last person who gets on the call, out of some misguided attempt to seem more important than everyone else, and you'll have to delicately balance getting your boss on the call last while still making sure your boss doesn't appear to be late. And if your boss does appear to be late, it will of course be your fault.

Example: Jimmy's boss has a habit of making other phone calls right when conference calls are scheduled to begin, so he always sets them for ten minutes later than the time his boss thinks they're scheduled for.

Call Dropping *(Failures)*

I will not try to drop a call on someone late at night and then get mad at you when that person actually picks up, forcing me to have an actual conversation.

Priorities *(Never Quite in Order)*

I will not call you into my office to talk to you about something and then, when my phone rings, ask, "Why aren't you answering my phones?" forcing you to sprint back to your desk to answer a call from someone I didn't want to speak to anyway.

Immediacy *(Confusing)*

I will not text you over the weekend to "call me immediately" and then not answer when you call back within seconds, forcing you to leave an awkward voice mail or risk annoying me by dialing repeatedly.

Rolling Calls *(While Eating)*

I will not roll calls while scarfing down lunch at my desk. I may not care about you or my peers, but I will at least have enough self-respect to keep the wet, disgusting sounds of my chewing from being amplified over the phone.

Weekend Conference Calls, Part 1

I won't make you drive to the office on a weekend just so you can conference me onto a call "the way I like it." If I can dial you on the office line a hundred times a day, I can figure out how to use a dial-in number you set up.

Weekend Conference Calls, Part 2

If I'm in a different time zone and set up a weekend conference call that starts at 4 A.M. your time, I will not make you wake up for it "just to make sure things go okay." We're all grown-ups here. We can handle a simple conference call without the supervision of a twenty-five-year-old.

Mobile Phones *(Placement)*

When you make a joke about keeping your BlackBerry next to your pillow so you can hear it buzz in your sleep, I will laugh at the ridiculousness of the idea instead of saying, "You don't do that?"

Scheduling
(Unnecessary Complications)

I will not impatiently tell you to "just call" someone, when the reason that you were trying to do it by e-mail was the six or seven complicated scheduling questions you need to ask, which will almost certainly result in at least one misunderstanding when you try to relay them over the phone.

Interruptions
(Counterproductive)

I will not stand over your shoulder and listen in on your side of a phone conversation with another assistant, interjecting with what I think you should be saying, thereby confusing you so much that you end up hanging up on the call without actually accomplishing what I had asked you to do.

Rolling Calls *(Tricking You into)*

I will not call you on your mobile over the weekend, claiming that I "can't find" someone's phone number in my contacts, ask you to connect me to that person on my mobile phone, and then segue that one call into an hour of you rolling calls for me as I try various friends and catering companies while coordinating a party I'm having next month.

Interruptions *(Aggressively Embarrassing)*

When another assistant calls you to ask you a question, I will not suddenly jump on the line and shout, "Who is this?" causing you to have to awkwardly explain that someone actually called wanting to talk to you instead of me.

Phone Skills *(Leaving Them to You for Both Our Sakes)*

I will not try to conference another line onto a call myself if I don't actually know how to do it, and then accidentally hang up on everyone and find a way to blame you for it.

Including You *(in the Worst Way Possible)*

While I'm on a conference call with multiple important people, waiting for one more person to join, I will not insist that you hop on the line and tell everyone "that funny story about [the time you embarrassed yourself horribly on your second day on the job, which was two years ago]."

Sanitation *(Unnecessary)*

I will not make you spend ten minutes every morning wiping down my entire phone with anti-bacterial wipes, even though I'm the only person who ever uses it.

Superstition *(Absurd)*

After we move offices, I will not make you spend an entire day begging the person in charge of our phone system to change my extension because it contains the number *13*.

Destruction *(of the Thing That Makes Me Able to Conduct Business)*

I will not rip my phone from its cord and/or throw it against the wall with such frequency that it becomes necessary for you to keep a drawer full of spare parts in your desk, so that you can repair it immediately, rather than spending the fifteen minutes it takes for IT to get upstairs listening to me yell at you about how whatever it was that caused me to break the phone was all your fault.

Phone Etiquette (Absence of)

When I'm talking to someone on the phone and you let me know that someone more important is calling on the other line, I will not abruptly hang up on the other person with no explanation, leaving you to make feeble excuses for my rude behavior to the angry executive on the line. I will be confident enough to trust that the second person will take my call in five minutes when I call back.

Tests (Embarrassing)

When I get a new mobile, I will not test its camera by taking twenty-five unflattering pictures of you sitting at your desk and then "accidentally" post them all to Facebook and tag them with your name.

Tones of Voice
(Oversensitivity to)

I will not accuse you of answering the phones in an "unfriendly" tone of voice and suggest that as the reason why I haven't been receiving as many calls as usual, even though you've been answering my phones the exact same way for the past two years, and it's pretty obvious the reason I'm not receiving many calls these days is that it's the time of the year when our business is notoriously slow, and I accuse you of the same thing every year.

Imitation (Best Form of Confusion)

I will not decide that I like the iPhone cover you have and make you order me the same one, so that now I always think the phone on your desk is my phone and constantly call you into my office because "my phone won't unlock!" due to the fact that I picked yours up off your desk again.

Answering the Phone
(Doing It Myself)

If the phone rings while you're away from your desk, doing something that I asked you to do, I will answer it myself, rather than allowing it to go to voice mail and then yelling at you for "making me" miss a call from someone I wanted to speak to.

Expenses *(Shady)*

I will not make you itemize my iPhone games apps on my expense reports as "research," especially if you have to plead with me to allow you to bill your mileage to the company when you run errands for me.

Your Phone Accessories
(Disgusting Destruction of)

I will not borrow your iPhone earbuds and return them to you coated in earwax.

Voice Mails *(Interminable)*

I will not call you on your office phone during lunch, try to hang up when I realize that you're not at your desk, and then leave a fifteen-minute recording on your voice mail of the noises of my pocket while I drive/walk/sit down to eat/use the restroom, to which you have to listen all the way through in order to delete it, due to the antique nature of our company's phone system.

Speaking on the Phone
(Being Prepared to)

When I call you on your mobile over the weekend, I will actually be in a position to talk to you when you answer, instead of having to spend forty-five seconds fumbling with the phone to get it to my mouth, causing you to think I've pocket-dialed you and hang up on the call, which I will then yell at you about.

Voice Mail Messages
(Unnecessary Perfectionism About Things I Should Just Do Myself)

I will not make you rerecord the voice mail message on my line fifteen times, insisting that your performance is "just not quite smooth enough," as if that has anything to do with how many people call me or what kind of messages they leave.

Competition
(Counterproductive)

I will not try to beat you to answering the phone when you

let it go for longer than one ring, and then wonder, very loudly, "What's the point of having an assistant, anyway?"

Finding My Mobile Phone
(Useless Ideas)

I will not make you call my mobile phone so that I can find it, insisting that "I just had it five minutes ago," when the reason I had it five minutes ago was that you were showing me how to put the ringer on silent.

Ringtones *(Repetition)*

I will not spend a full thirty minutes trying to decide between mobile ring tones, playing them over and over again at top volume until you're just about ready to run into my office, grab the phone from my hand, and smash it under your foot.

Thinking *(Over the Phone)*

I will not call you on the office line after I've left work for the day, say, "Oh, I forgot what I wanted to tell you," and then make you wait on the line while I try to remember what it was, when all you want to do is pack up and go home.

Ringtones *(Insulting)*

I will not ask you to show me how to set special ringtones for different people in my phone contacts, and then later inform you that I've set yours to be the sound of a bird chirping, "because that's what it sounds like when you bother me all day with your questions."

Unknown Numbers
(Impossibility of ESP)

I will not call you over the weekend from a number you don't recognize because I can't find my phone and have to use a friend's in order to call you to ask you where it could possibly be, and then get mad at you when you don't answer right away.

Ringtones *(Theft of)*

After I decide that I like your phone's ringtone, I will not use it for my own phone and tell you to pick a new one, because "otherwise it will be too confusing for me."

Phone Etiquette *(Passing the Buck)*

When I accidentally cough, burp, or sneeze into the phone's receiver while on a call, I will not blame it on you, making a big show of yelling at you for not having your phone on mute.

Call Waiting *(and Waiting, and Waiting, and Waiting)*

When I'm talking to you from my mobile, and someone calls me on the other line, I will not try and fail repeatedly to switch to the other call, getting angrier and angrier at you every time I say "Hello?" and am greeted with your voice, telling me that it's still you on the line, as if you are intentionally sabotaging my ability to speak to other people.

Indecision *(Costly)*

I will not insist that you call me from your mobile over the weekend when I'm in a foreign country and then refuse to pay you back for the fifteen minutes I spent trying to make up my mind about which restaurant I should go to for breakfast two days from now, while you listened and tried to calculate how much more of your paycheck it will take for me to make a decision.

Mobile Phone Use *(Making Up My Mind)*

I will not insist that you keep your mobile in a drawer when you're at work, "to make sure you don't get distracted," and then yell at you for not immediately answering the texts I send you from my colleague's office, asking for you to bring me a certain piece of paper.

New Phones *(Priorities)*

After insisting that the company just doesn't have the money to get you a new work BlackBerry with a keyboard that does not require you to press certain buttons five times for them to work, I will not then segue into a request for you to order my twelve-year-old child a brand-new iPhone.

Blame (Really Committing to)

When I accidentally hang up on someone I'm talking to, I will not have you get that person back on the phone, blame you for the interruption, insisting that you disconnected us, and then make you get on the line to apologize to the person I hung up on and promise that it will never happen again (it will, because I don't know how to use my phone).

Availability by Phone (Lack of Control over)

I will not tell you to "try everyone on the call sheet" and then get mad at you when the only person who picks up is the one person I didn't want to talk to, as if you arranged things to happen that way on purpose.

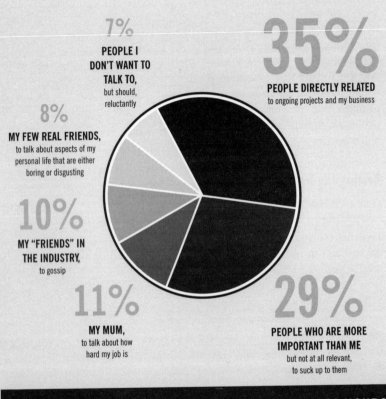

7%

PEOPLE I DON'T WANT TO TALK TO, but should, reluctantly

35%

PEOPLE DIRECTLY RELATED to ongoing projects and my business

8%

MY FEW REAL FRIENDS, to talk about aspects of my personal life that are either boring or disgusting

10%

MY "FRIENDS" IN THE INDUSTRY, to gossip

11%

MY MUM, to talk about how hard my job is

29%

PEOPLE WHO ARE MORE IMPORTANT THAN ME but not at all relevant, to suck up to them

PEOPLE I WILL ACTUALLY CALL DURING BUSINESS HOURS
A Breakdown

IMs FROM HELL: **NUMBERS**
(Using Them to Tell Things Apart)

2:34 P.M.

Sam Towson on line 1,
Alexandra Peters on line 2.

 ASSISTANT

2:35 P.M.

 BOSS

I'll take Sam

2:35 P.M.

He's on line 1

 ASSISTANT

2:35 P.M.

That's line 2

 ASSISTANT

2:36 P.M.

That's still line 2

 ASSISTANT

2:36 P.M.

you're still on line 2
—Sam is on line 1

 ASSISTANT
 ASSISTANT

2:37 P.M.

 BOSS

tell Sam I'll call
him right back

2:38 P.M.

BOSS

don't ever let this
happen again

E-MAIL, INSTANT MESSAGING, AND TEXTING

They Were Supposed to Make Life Easier, Right?

Instant Messaging *(It's Not Quite the Same as Speaking)*

I will never IM you a question and then IM it to you again in all caps, over and over again, with increasingly frantic punctuation, if you don't answer it immediately.

Types of Communication *(Picking the Best One)*

When I'm out of the office, I will not insist on working out the logistics of a very important meeting by a convoluted, hour-long text exchange, rather than just picking up the phone and having a five-minute conversation with you.

Important Conversations *(Appropriate Delivery of)*

I will not fire you by text, e-mail, or over the phone. If I can't bear to sit down face-to-face and talk it out with you, I'm too much of a wimp to earn the privilege of firing someone.

E-mail *(Paying Attention)*

If I'm gossiping about someone in an e-mail, I will not accidentally CC that person on that very e-mail and then find a way to blame it entirely on you.

E-mail Signatures
(Hypocritical)

I will not have you add a line to my e-mail signature that says, "Please consider the environment before printing this e-mail," but continue to make you print out and file all the e-mails I consider important (which is basically every e-mail I've ever received from a person instead of an e-mail subscription list), "just in case something happens with the computer."

Proofreading *(Excessive)*

After discovering that you are quite good at grammar and spelling, I will not call you into my office to look over almost every single e-mail I send out, and then wonder why you're not getting things done as fast as you used to. I'll use spell-checker or the last useful remnants of my college education instead.

Understanding E-mail Functions, Part 1

I will not BCC you on an e-mail and then ask you to Reply All to it with your contact information, "in case people need your help," forcing you to suddenly appear on an e-mail chain out of nowhere and appear to be creepy, incompetent, or both.

Understanding E-mail Functions, Part 2

I will understand the difference between Forward and Reply, as well as the fact that one of these actions results in the attachment I want printed being sent to you and the other does not.

Understanding E-mail Functions, Part 3

I will understand that e-mail attachments can only be so big, and that my e-mail is not "broken" when it's unable to send a fifty-megabyte video file to my best friend (who probably didn't want to get a fifteen-minute, unedited video of my dog doing basic tricks anyway).

E-mail Signatures *(Annoying to Everyone Involved)*

If I insist on including inspirational quotes in my e-mail signatures, I will find them myself. I will not put you in charge of finding just the right upbeat saying every week and switching out the old one before I come into the office on Monday morning.

Advertising *(Embarrassing)*

I will not make you send out an all-staff e-mail to advertise a "blowout sale!" at the extremely expensive doggie clothing boutique my family member works at part-time.

The Loop *(Keeping You in)*

I will not constantly forget to CC you on e-mails, and then later get angry at you when you can't find the very important e-mail I insist that I included you on.

Subject Lines *(Importance of Completing)*

I will actually type the subject of my e-mails to you into the subject line of the e-mail, so that you can easily find which one I'm yelling for you to find "NOW NOW NOW" while I'm on a conference call. I will not leave the subject lines of all my e-mails to you blank, so that you end up having to forward them to yourself with a new subject line, a task that seems easy enough until you consider the fact that I send you about five hundred e-mails per day.

Organization *(Pointless)*

When you organize all my e-mails into folders so that I can find important messages more easily, per my request, and spend a good half hour explaining to me how to drag e-mails into folders myself, and how to find things, I will not call you into my office the next day and insist that "you deleted most of my inbox!"

Texting *(with a Toddler)*

I will not regularly allow my young child to play with my

iPhone, resulting in you receiving frequent texts from "me" after work hours and on weekends that consist of strings of nonsensical characters and emoticons (which nonetheless cause your heart rate to skyrocket every time my name pops up on your phone).

IMs *(Stands for "Interrupting Messages")*

When you're working on an important project that needs to be done within the next two hours, I will not IM you a series of questions about other completely unimportant tasks that need to be done within the next month, because I'm bored due to the fact that you're doing all my work for me.

Mistaken Identity *(Blame for)*

I will not carry out an entire IM conversation with you believing that you're someone else, and then, when I realize my mistake, get mad at you for "deceiving me," even though you had no idea what was happening due to the general incoherence of the IMs I actually do intend to send to you.

Autocorrect *(or Autoconfuse)*

I will pay attention to my phone's autocorrect function and realize when it changes my messages into incomprehensible haiku-like collections of words. I will not get mad at you when you fail to understand these haiku and ask me to clarify.

E-mail *(Unsent and Therefore Unseen)*

I will not make a habit of saving unsent e-mails to you in my drafts folder to finish up at a later time, and then scream at you when you don't do what I told you to do in those e-mails, because I never actually sent or even finished them.

Self-Reference *(Annoying and Slightly Unsettling)*

I will not frequently refer to myself in the third person when IMing, e-mailing, or texting you. I am not royalty, nor do I even behave well enough to think that I am.

Instructions *(Complete Lack of)*

I will not forward you e-mails from people you've never heard of talking about seemingly random subjects with no context whatsoever, and then, after you've replied asking for some clarification, respond only with the words "Did u handle????"

Punctuation *(Infuriating)*

I will not end every sentence I type to you with an ellipsis "..." so that you constantly feel as if I'm either expecting you to say more or implying that what you've just written to me is completely obvious and useless.

Decision Making *(Farming Out Unnecessarily)*

I will not sign up for ten different daily coupon e-mail lists and then forward you each e-mail I receive from them every morning, so you can "research" all the deals and give me a report on which ones might be worth my buying, even though I have never purchased a single one in the eight months I've been making you do this for me.

Typing *(Time-Wasting)*

I will not IM you the full text of an e-mail I want you to send to someone from my e-mail address. If I can type the text into an IM chat window, I can type it into an e-mail and send it myself, especially if you're already trying to get something done for me within the next fifteen minutes.

Respect *(Two-Way)*

I will not insist that you sign every e-mail you send to me (and only me) with the words "Best, [your name]," because "it's a sign of respect," even though I frequently send you e-mails in all caps with no regard for punctuation, spelling, coherence, or etiquette.

Emoticons *(Confusing)*

I will not send you what seems to be a completely straightforward and sincere e-mail and then sign it with a winking emoticon ";)" causing you to become unsure if what I wrote is meant to be taken at face value or if you're supposed to read some mysterious second meaning into it.

E-mail Signatures
(Unnecessary Judgment of)

When you CC me on an e-mail you've sent to another assistant, I will not question if your signature of "Cheers" is perhaps too informal, despite the fact that I consistently sign my own e-mails with "Hugs," "xx," and "xoxo," believing myself to be keeping up with the times.

Overthinking Things (a Luxury Allowed for Only Me)

I will not spend two hours agonizing over the word choice of an e-mail I need to send, asking for and then disregarding your opinion, but then, when you ask me to look over a sensitive e-mail you'll be sending to someone important on my behalf, say, "Stop overanalyzing and just send it already!"

E-mail Forwarding
(Betrayals)

When we have an e-mail exchange that consists mostly of making fun of a colleague of ours, followed by a brief discussion of times that would work for me to have a meeting with said colleague, I will not forward to that colleague the last e-mail in that chain, which includes not only the potential meeting times we came up with but also a transcript of all the jokes about him or her we were able to come up with, which, when I discover what I've done, I will blame entirely on you.

E-mail Addresses (Unknown)

I will not get mad at you when you fail to set up the personal Hotmail e-mail address you never knew I had on my brand-new smartphone, causing me to be deprived of update e-mails from my online dating service/fantasy sports league/discount shopping website for a full sixteen hours.

Screen Names (Awkward, Unprofessional, and Completely Inaccurate)

I will not have an IM screen name that is similar to "Stud1234," "Hottie4321," "Babe9876," "6Pack4567," or any variation thereof.

Paragraphs *(Perfectly Normal Formatting)*

When you send me an e-mail that consists of two or more paragraphs, broken up by spaces between said paragraphs, I will not read only the first paragraph and then insist that your "weird formatting" made me think that you were done after your first few sentences, though the content clearly indicates that you were not.

Answers *(Hieroglyphic)*

I will not respond to things you're asking me over IM with only smiley faces or frowny faces, turning simple yes-or-no questions into an exercise of guessing which answer makes me happy and which makes me sad.

Access to My E-mail Account *(Downsides to, Part 1)*

I will not make a habit of e-mailing "sexy" things to my spouse on my work e-mail account, which you have full access to and frequently have to look through to find e-mails that I've "lost."

Access to My E-mail Account *(Downsides to, Part 2)*

I will not send one of my colleagues/friends an e-mail from my work e-mail account, which, again, you have full access to and look through frequently, detailing all your (perfectly normal) personality traits that annoy me, and wonder what the best way to fire you "without actually firing" you is if they become "too much for me to handle."

Access to My E-mail Account *(Downsides to, Part 3)*

After I discover that you can send e-mails from my e-mail address on your own computer, I will not get into the habit of sending you a few incoherent sentences and an e-mail address whenever I don't feel like making the effort of typing out my full thoughts myself, and expect you to write and send an e-mail that makes perfect sense and sounds like I wrote it myself. I'll save this e-mail feature for emergencies only, so that you don't have to be responsible for the e-mails of two people.

Sound *(Importance of)*

If I ask you to turn the sound of your instant messaging program off because it's annoying me, I will not then get mad at you later when you don't answer my IMs immediately because you can't hear them.

Profile Pictures *(Inaccurate Representations of Personality)*

I will not set my IM profile picture to be that of an adorable animal, so that when I'm lecturing you over instant message, my unnecessarily sharp words appear to be coming from a wide-eyed kitten or puppy, a confusing combination of words and images that has the effect of causing you to shiver whenever you see a picture of a cute animal on the Internet for months after you've stopped working for me.

Sarcasm *(Proper Use of)*

I will understand that the barely tolerable sarcasm I use so frequently in my face-to-face conversations with you, which I find to be hilarious, does not translate so well to the written word, and causes many of my e-mails, IMs, and texts to be confusing, slightly off-putting, or both.

Your Opinion *(Revealing What I Think of)*

I will not forward you an e-mail from someone else, asking, "What do you think?" and then, after you reply with a well-reasoned and helpful breakdown of what you think about the matter, respond to let you know that I meant to forward it to someone else, which should have been obvious to you, since I would never ask your opinion on such an important matter.

EXPECTATION VS. REALITY

*Methods of Communication—
the Right One for the Situation,
and the One I Will Actually Use*

THE SITUATION	THE APPROPRIATE METHOD OF COMMUNICATION	THE METHOD OF COMMUNICATION I WILL USE
You're on the phone, trying to get a top-priority meeting scheduled, and I want you to convey something to the other assistant.	Going to my desk and IMing you that information, because I know that you always have an eye on your IM window.	Standing behind you and repeating that information over and over again when there's a pause in your side of the conversation, resulting in your inability to understand both me and the person on the line.

THE SITUATION	THE APPROPRIATE METHOD OF COMMUNICATION	THE METHOD OF COMMUNICATION I WILL USE
It's a weekend, and I need you to do something that requires a good amount of explanation from me for you to be able to do it correctly.	Sending you an e-mail outlining what I need you to do, and, if it's urgent, a text asking you to please check your e-mail.	Leaving you a five-minute-long voice mail, in which I try and fail to clearly explain what I need you to do, and then failing to answer my phone or email for the next four hours while you try to get some much-needed clarity.
Something is annoying me, but I can't make you come into my office and listen to me complain about it, because you're currently working on a time-sensitive project that I asked you to do.	Waiting until you're done with the project (at which point I probably will have forgotten what was annoying me anyway), or going to find someone of lesser rank than me to complain to.	IMing you my complaints and expecting you to respond immediately to them with frowny faces and words of sympathy; accusing you of being "unable to multitask" when it takes you longer than five seconds to reply, due to the fact that you're concentrating on something that's actually important.
I have some notes to give you on a document you wrote.	Writing all the notes on the document in a legible hand and handing the annotated document to you for revisions.	Scribbling notes on the first copy of the document I can find in the pile of papers on my desk, which will inevitably be a two-week-old draft that we've revised multiple times, and then yelling at you when you let me know that I have to do the notes all over again.

IMs FROM HELL: **INSTANT MESSAGING**

(Not a Portable Method of Communication)

1:05 P.M.

 BOSS James

1:05 P.M.

 BOSS JAMES

1:06 P.M.

 BOSS JAMES

1:07 P.M.

 BOSS James where are you???????????????

1:07 P.M.

BOSS ???????!!!1!!???????

1:08 P.M.

BOSS AJMESS!!?!?!!!!!

1:09 P.M.

Sorry, I was grabbing
that document
you wanted from
the printer **ASSISTANT**

1:09 P.M.

 BOSS my water carafe is empty

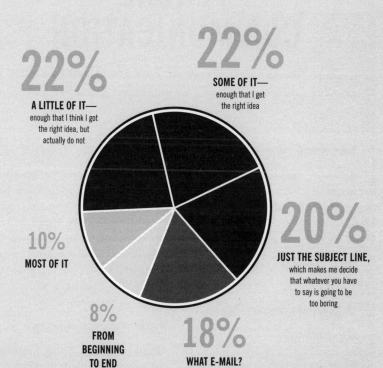

22%

A LITTLE OF IT—
enough that I think I got
the right idea, but
actually do not

22%

SOME OF IT—
enough that I get
the right idea

10%

MOST OF IT

20%

JUST THE SUBJECT LINE,
which makes me decide
that whatever you have
to say is going to be
too boring

8%

**FROM
BEGINNING
TO END**

18%

WHAT E-MAIL?

HOW MUCH OF THE E-MAIL YOU SENT ME I WILL ACTUALLY READ
A Breakdown

VERBAL COMMUNICATION

Had You Wanted to Spend This Much Time Pulling
Teeth, You'd Have Gone to Dental School

Your Name *(Wearing It Out)*

When I call your name from inside my office and you don't answer, I'll assume that you're away from your desk or talking to someone on the phone. I won't just keep saying your name over and over again until you respond.

Nonverbal Communication

(Degrading)

I will not make clicking or whistling noises to indicate that you should follow me somewhere, as if you were a horse or a dog.

Questions *(Fake Answers to)*

When you ask me a question about something, my answer will be more than a sentence that consists of your original question in statement form, plus the words "you know what I mean" in the place of where the crucial information is supposed to go.

Anger *(Condescending)*

When I'm angry at you, I will not call you by both your first and last names to indicate so, as if I am your mother, father, or teacher.

Explanations (Redundant)

I will not ask you to explain to me in detail how a certain piece of technology works, and, after you've spent fifteen minutes doing so, say, "Great. Now type that into an e-mail so I can understand it."

Answers (Delayed Indefinitely)

When you walk into my office to ask me an important question that I've ignored on both e-mail and IM, I will not accuse you of being too aggressive and tell you that "I'll get back to you when I get back to you," even though we both know that means "never."

Your Name (Not Caring About It at All)

I will not regularly call you by my previous assistant's name, never really bothering to make the switch, so that you find yourself answering to someone else's name on a daily basis, confusing everyone in the office for the first month you work there (especially if you and my previous assistant are different genders).

Ambushes (Lengthy)

I will not suddenly appear behind you in the hallway and start describing a project to you in detail, not allowing you the time to run to your desk to grab a pen and pad of paper so that you can actually remember all the weird specifications I'm throwing at you a mile a minute.

Nicknames (Icky)

I will not call you "honey," "sweetheart," "dear," or any other variation of those terms. I am not your parent, your significant other, or a middle-aged waitress.

Statements (Undermining)

I will not say, "You look tired," right before you're supposed to make a presentation to the entire company.

Manners (Basic)

I will say "please" and "thank you" rather than barking orders and accepting the things you bring me in resentful silence.

Conversation
(Normal Formation of)

When I come out of my office to talk to you about something, I will stand in front of your desk and talk to your face. I will not come around and stand behind your desk, forcing you to turn your head but not your chair, because I'm standing so close to you that to swivel your chair around would mean your knees brushing up against mine.

Apologies *(Forced Repetition of)*

After you've made a mistake and apologized for it, and I've accepted your apology and ostensibly forgiven you, I will not then spend the rest of the week haranguing you about that same mistake, forcing you to apologize over and over and over again until you have even less self-esteem than I do.

Names *(Pronunciation)*

If I cannot for the life of me pronounce a certain colleague's name correctly, I will not get mad at you for correcting me when I say it incorrectly out of anyone else's earshot, then become even more furious when you stop correcting me and I butcher that colleague's name in front of the whole company.

Your Opinion *(Actually Wanting It When I Ask for It)*

When I ask for your opinion on something, I will not accuse you of lacking originality when you agree with me and of being purposefully contradictory when you disagree.

Being a Poet *(Without Knowing It)*

I will not get mad at you for chuckling when four sentences I say to you accidentally rhyme perfectly in iambic pentameter. I'll laugh, too, because I have a sense of humor, and what I just said does sound ridiculous.

Answers *(Spoken Out Loud)*

When you ask me a question, I will not offer you a shrug as my only answer. I'll at least make the effort to say "I don't know," especially if this conversation is taking place while we're both sitting at our desks and therefore can't actually see each other.

Tones of Voice *(False Alarms)*

I will not make a habit of calling you into my office in a very serious tone of voice only to discuss something completely frivolous with you, so that you worry that I'm going to fire you almost every other day of the week.

Distances *(Communication over)*

I will not yell your name from the other end of the office and expect you to be able to hear me and respond. I'll call you on the phone instead, making proper use of a device that was invented to solve exactly the problem of communication over non-shoutable distances.

Sentences *(Allowing Completion of)*

When we're having a conversation, I will let you finish your sentences, rather than taking just the first four words out of your mouth as a complete answer and then insisting that you're wrong.

Questions *(Answering with)*

I will not answer a simple yes-or-no question with a question of my own, an exercise I think will help lead you to the answer yourself, but which only results in confusion and delay.

Tones of Voice *(Using Different Ones for Different Occasions)*

My "sarcastic, angry voice" will not be the same deadpan tone as my "neutral, question-answering voice," forcing you to turn almost every conversation into one that annoys me due to your constant need for confirmation that I actually meant what I said.

Answers *(Canceling Out)*

When I ask you a question, and you reply with an "Ummmmm" noise while you consider the answer, I will not repeat that noise back to you in a loud, aggressive tone, ostensibly to suggest that you stop responding to questions that way, but with the result of making you flustered and unable to answer my question correctly.

Professionalism
(Imagined Problems with)

I will not suggest that you "get rid of" your very slight regional accent "so you sound more professional."

Swearing *(Hypocrisy)*

I will not swear constantly, at everyone and everything, but shoot you a look of shocked disapproval when you allow a "damn!" to slip from your mouth after you give yourself a two-inch paper cut on your thumb.

Thanks *(Said but Not Meant)*

Whenever I actually say "thanks" to you, I will not say it in a tone of voice that is so sarcastic that it implies exactly the opposite.

Exclamations *(Confounding)*

After you successfully complete a project or task for me, I will not exclaim, "That's why I pay you the big bucks!" when I know that you make £10 an hour, with limited overtime.

Interruptions *(of Myself, by Myself)*

I will not interrupt myself in the middle of a thought when something else occurs to me and then refuse to go back to what I was saying before, insisting that "you have enough to go on," due to the fact that I can't actually remember what I was talking about before and don't want to reveal that weakness to you.

Slang *(Horrific)*

I will not combine every outdated slang word I happen to overhear into a mishmash of horribly misappropriated cultural garbage that causes you to want to crawl under your desk and hide whenever you hear me start a phone conversation with the words "What's up, bro dog? How are you hanging today? LOL!"

Dictation *(Unnecessary Repetition of)*

I will not make you take dictation, have you read back to me the words, which you've transcribed perfectly, say, "No, no, no—you wrote it down all wrong. Are you deaf?" and then dictate a "new" document to you, which has exactly the same meaning as the first one with a slightly different choice of words.

Yelling *(Confusing)*

I will not watch sports games on my computer without telling you and then shout unintelligible syllables at the screen, causing you to run into my office whenever someone scores or doesn't score, since there's really no difference between my sports yells and my angry yells.

Answers *(Unhelpful and Insulting)*

If I'm in a bad mood, I might close the door to my office for a few minutes to regroup and calm down. I will not, however, choose to express my bad mood by answering any questions you ask me in a sneering, sniveling, fake-whiny tone of voice that makes you feel like an idiot for daring to ask me something perfectly reasonable.

Tones of Voice *(Unnecessarily Insulting)*

When I'm explaining something to you, I will not automatically switch over to a condescending tone of voice that implies I'm speaking to a child, even if you haven't asked me any "annoying" questions yet.

Responsibility *(Sudden Sharing of)*

When discussing a project that we both worked on during a company meeting, I will not start out describing the process with sentences that begin with the word *I*, then, as people ask more and more probing and critical questions, switch to statements that start with the word *we*.

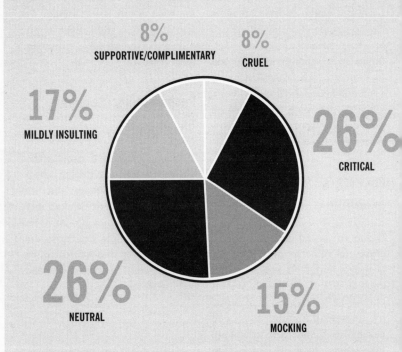

8%
SUPPORTIVE/COMPLIMENTARY

8%
CRUEL

17%
MILDLY INSULTING

26%
CRITICAL

26%
NEUTRAL

15%
MOCKING

CONTENT OF THE WORDS THAT I SAY TO YOU
A Breakdown

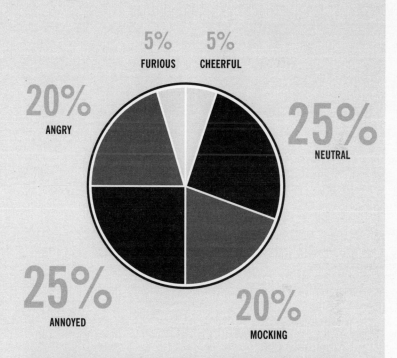

5% **FURIOUS**
5% **CHEERFUL**
20% **ANGRY**
25% **NEUTRAL**
25% **ANNOYED**
20% **MOCKING**

TONE OF THE WORDS THAT I SAY TO YOU
A Breakdown

4

TRAVEL
and
TRANSPORTATION

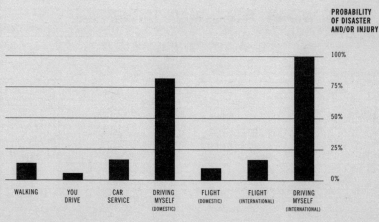

PROBABILITY
OF DISASTER
AND/OR INJURY

100%

75%

50%

25%

0%

WALKING | YOU DRIVE | CAR SERVICE | DRIVING MYSELF (DOMESTIC) | FLIGHT (DOMESTIC) | FLIGHT (INTERNATIONAL) | DRIVING MYSELF (INTERNATIONAL)

METHOD OF TRANSPORTATION

TRAVEL

*Normal People Really Do Not Have
This Much Trouble with It*

15%

I'M CONVINCED THAT THE PLACE
is going to be the next hotspot for rich people, and I want to be the first of my friends to visit, so that when they excitedly tell me that they plan to travel there, I can say, "Oh, [Name of Place]? It was great six months ago, but now that people know about it . . ."

40%

I'M ABLE TO MAKE UP A BUSINESS-RELATED REASON FOR GOING THERE,
so I may as well go, on expenses, of course

11%

THE PERSON I'M CHEATING ON MY SPOUSE WITH LIVES THERE

6%

I HAVE A REAL, BUSINESS-RELATED REASON TO GO THERE,
and won't be spending a penny more of the company's money than I need to

22%

ONE OF MY COLLEAGUES WENT THERE
on holiday a month ago, and I can't let him or her be more well travelled than I am

6%

I'VE WANTED TO VISIT THE PLACE FOR A LONG TIME,
and finally feel like I can reward myself with a vacation there

MY REASONS FOR TRAVELING SOMEWHERE
A Breakdown

Travel Agents (Usefulness of)

I will not refuse to use our company's travel agent when booking flights, out of some strange sense of pride. I will understand that with less than half their knowledge, experience, and time, you won't be able to do as good a job as they do.

Travel Information (Nonessential)

I will not make you spend twenty minutes on hold with an airline's customer service to ask what kind of plane I'll be flying on, just because "I was hoping it would be one of the new ones."

Safety (Irrational Concerns About)

I will not insist that you get me an airfare as low as possible, and then, when you present me with a list of less-mainstream-but-still-reputable airlines that have the lowest fares (which you fly all the time), ask in all sincerity if you're trying to make me die in a plane crash.

Rental Cars (Procrastination)

I will not tell you to find me a specific sports car to rent during my travels, and then, when you send me the only two options that exist in the city I'm going to, take so long to decide which color I want that by the time you try to book the car, both of them have already been rented to other people.

Airplane Seats (Making a Choice)

I will not refuse to answer when you ask whether I'd rather sit in the window or aisle seat of a plane, and then complain about whichever choice you're forced to make for me.

Pet Travel (Ridiculous)

I will not ask you to get my overweight dog certified as a "psychiatric service animal" just so he can travel with me in the cabin on flights, forcing you to spend several hours on the phone, lying to a very kind person at the local disability office whose eagerness to help makes you feel all the guiltier for assisting me in scamming the system.

Great Deals (Impossibility of Finding by Oneself)

I will not ask you to find me a rental home for my holiday, turn down every single option you find as being either too ugly or too expensive, and then, after I find a place that belongs to a friend of mine, who will let me stay there for free, complain that "I have to do everything around here to get a good deal."

Flight Schedules (Expectations Versus Reality)

When you let me know that there is only one flight available during a twelve-hour window, I will not respond by forwarding you a previous e-mail of mine, in which I have underlined, bolded, and italicized the sentence in which I demanded multiple flight options.

Pet Travel (Deflecting Blame)

If I forget to tell you until the day before I travel that I intend to bring my small dog on the plane with me, and you then let me know that unfortunately the flight's pet reservations for the cabin are full, I will not tell you that I will consider you to be a murderer if something happens to "my baby" while she's traveling in the cargo hold.

Hotel Research (Unnecessary)

I will not make you spend almost a full day researching hotel options for me, printing out a thirty-page packet of detailed information on all of them, including lists and reviews of nearby restaurants and shops, and then, when you present it to me, flip through the first four pages and decide that I just want to book a room at the same place I always stay at when I visit that city.

Airline Miles (Exhausting Every Impossible and Unnecessary Option)

Every time I need to book a flight, I will not make you spend several hours trying to figure out how I can use my airline miles to try to get a free ticket, which is usually impossible since I always leave making decisions on travel plans till the very last minute, before finally allowing you to put the tickets on my credit card, which I will end up expensing to the company anyway.

Physical Distances
(Permanence of)

I will not ask if you can find a "shorter" flight from one location to another, when all the options you've provided me are already nonstop.

Time-Saving Schemes
(Grotesque)

I will not ask you to call the airline I'm flying on and pretend that I have a serious illness that requires me to be wheeled through the airport in a wheelchair, just so I can get through the security line a little faster.

Money-Saving Schemes
(Also Grotesque)

I will not make you call a hotel that I decided not to stay in at the last minute and "explain" that I've had a death in my family in an attempt to convince them not to charge me the cancellation fee.

Packing *(Painstaking and a Little Gross)*

I will not make you spend the afternoon before I travel pouring all of my strange-smelling "natural" luxury toiletries into regulation-sized travel bottles, yelling, "Careful—that's expensive!" every time I walk past your desk and believe you to be on the verge of spilling a single drop of the stuff, even though you've crafted a funnel out of a plastic folder and tape to make sure that none of the stuff ends up leaving your desk smelling like me.

Forgetfulness *(Untimely)*

I will not e-mail you at 9 the night before my 6 A.M. flight to say that I forgot to get an international converter for my electronics and can you please find a way to get one to me before I leave thank you.

Flight Check-ins
(Redundant Confirmation of)

I will not call you on your mobile phone at 6 A.M. to confirm that you already checked me in for my 10 A.M. flight, especially when I have an e-mail from you sitting at the top of my inbox from the previous night, which states that you have indeed done so.

Travel Budgets *(Hypocritical)*

I will not ask you to take me to the airport for my 7 A.M. flight, "because a car service is too expensive," and then in the same breath tell you to look into getting me an iPad for my trip so I don't have to carry any books around.

Preparation *(Tragically Forgotten)*

When I'm going on a multi-country business trip, and you make me a binder containing an itinerary, every piece of contact info I could possibly need, detailed maps, basic phrases in the languages of the countries I'm traveling to, and recommendations for restaurants of all price levels in the cities I'll be staying in, I will not leave the binder in the cab I took to the airport and then spend the entire trip calling or texting you every hour or two to ask where to go next.

Ancestry *(Limitations of)*

I will not expect you to know everything about a certain country just because your great-great-grandparents emigrated from there.

Passport Photos
(Unprofessional Retouching)

I will not bring you the pictures I had taken for my passport renewal and ask you to "do your magic" in Photoshop so that my ears don't stick out so much, when the only "magic" you've ever done in Photoshop was to take a really big image file and turn it into a smaller image file.

Travel Suggestions *(Not Snobby Enough for Me)*

When I decide to travel to a city in a country that you've visited before, and you excitedly tell me how much you loved it there and offer to give me some suggestions on museums, restaurants, and bars to visit, I will not thank you for your offer but then dismiss it, saying, "I think my trip there is going to be a little more upscale than yours was. I'm staying in a five-star hotel, not a hostel, for one thing," even though you never said you stayed in a hostel; I'm just making the assumption that you did.

Diets *(Restrictions of)*

When I'm planning a holiday, I will not make you call up all the restaurants near the resort where I'm staying and compile a list of which ones are willing to serve me plain grilled fish (three specific types only) and plain grilled vegetables, and then act surprised when your list consists of exactly one restaurant—the one inside the resort.

Being Adventurous
(Not Even a Little Bit)

I will not ask you to send me PDF's (in English) of the menus of every restaurant I'm planning to eat at during my vacation to rural Tuscany, "just so I can make sure there's something I like at all of them."

Fake-outs *(Cruel)*

I will not ask if you want to come with me on a business trip to a different country, and then, when you excitedly say yes, laugh and tell you I was just kidding, because "the company would never spend that kind of money on you!"

Communication Abilities
(Expectations of)

When I'm on the way to the airport to take an eight-hour flight, and you call me with an urgent problem that we need to deal with, I will not insist that "I'll take care of it on the plane," despite your repeatedly telling me that my flight does not have wireless, and then send you a series of furious e-mails when I land, accusing you of "willfully sabotaging my productivity."

Airplane Wireless *(Abuse of)*

When there's wireless on one of my flights, I will use it to watch Netflix and read online newspapers. I will not use it to harass you via e-mail and instant message during the six hours that you thought you were completely free from me and were hoping to use to finally get some work done.

Airplane Rules *(Anticipating)*

I won't roll calls with you on a plane up until the point when the flight attendant wrestles my phone from my hands, and then blame you for not getting the most important call in time, which of course I've left until the last minute.

Flight Delays
(Impossible Solutions for)

When my flight is delayed due to mechanical difficulties, I will not call and tell you to hold multiple flights on the same airline under fake names to guarantee I get seats. When you politely explain that this is impossible, I will not yell, "Fine! I'll do it myself!" which we both know is not going to happen, due to the fact that I haven't booked my own travel in more than ten years.

Micromanaging *(from Thirty-five Thousand Feet)*

I will not make you spend several hours loading my iPad with movies, books, and music for my five-hour flight, and then spend the entire trip IMing you over the airplane's wireless to remind you to do tasks that you would have already completed, were it not for the fact that you have to stop what you're doing every five minutes to reply to my messages.

Complaints *(for the Sake of Complaining)*

I will not call you before my flight takes off to complain about the fact that the tickets you bought me are on an overbooked flight, which you had no way of knowing, especially when the result was that I got bumped up from business class to first.

Jet Lag *(Instantaneous?)*

I will not promise to work on a project that you've been trying to get me to finish for weeks on my eight-hour flight, "since I won't have anything better to do!" and then instead choose to get drunk on tiny bottles of booze, watch a few hours of terrible TV on the airplane's entertainment center, pass out for the remainder of the flight, wake up when the plane touches down so hungover that the only thing I can concentrate on is getting to my hotel and sleeping for a full twelve hours, and then try to blame my poor choices on "jet lag," as if it happens as soon as one steps onto a jet.

Airplanes *(Not Quite the Same Rules as My Office)*

If we're both traveling by plane on a business trip, and I'm in business class and you're in economy (naturally), I will not IM you every five minutes over the airplane's wireless to "come and see me" so I can tell you something I'm too lazy to type into the IM chat window, making you walk up to my seat in the business-class cabin so frequently that the flight attendants eventually threaten to have you restrained.

Seat Assignments *(Impossible Predictions)*

I will not e-mail you from the two-hour flight I'm currently on, asking if, next time you book me a ticket, you could please make sure I won't be sitting next to "a fatty."

Lost Luggage *(Blame)*

I will not blame you when my luggage gets lost on a flight you booked with an airline I told you was "really the best out of all of them."

Google *(Limits of)*

I will not call you from a city in a foreign country that you've never been to and say, "Find me a good place for dinner tonight. Somewhere the locals go, no tourists, but make sure the waiters understand English. And make sure they have a vegan option available in case I feel like it. Also, I want to eat in an hour, so make sure it's near [intersection of two streets that I mispronounce horribly and refuse to repeat]. Thanks bye!"

International Phone Service
(Unpredictability of)

When I decide to take a hip holiday to a beautiful out-of-the-way country, even though my constitution is completely unsuited to any kind of dirt, delay, or unusual foodstuffs, I will not spend my first three days there e-mailing you in all caps on my laptop from my hotel room because my Black-Berry is not working and I'm afraid to be away from my e-mail for more than ten minutes.

Obscurity *(Not Always an Indication of Quality)*

When visiting a foreign country on holiday, I will not discount every restaurant, museum, or attraction you suggest as being "too touristy," just because you were able to find out about it.

Trains *(and Class Warfare)*

When you suggest that the easiest way to get from Point A to Point B might be to take a train, I will not laugh in your face and ask if you "think I'm a peasant."

Weather *(Predictability of)*

I will not get mad at you when it rains during my travels and the many pages of exhaustive weather reports you printed out for me prior to my departure didn't predict it. Especially when I'm traveling in the UK and you advised me to pack a raincoat despite the sunny forecast, but I refused.

Freebies *(Whining About)*

I will not call you from my hotel room to complain about the quality of the complimentary fruit basket that was waiting for me when I arrived at my executive suite.

Bragging *(Torturous)*

When on a business trip in a different country, I will not e-mail you five pictures per night on average of the beautiful scenery, delicious food, and deadly-looking drinks I'm enjoying. I will recognize that, due to the time difference, this will cause you to be woken up by the buzzing of your BlackBerry throughout the night, and that it is ridiculous for me to make you lose sleep so I can brag at you.

Customs *(Existence of)*

I will not tell you to FedEx my iPad, Kindle, or other electronic device to me while I'm in a foreign country, ignore all of your warnings about how long it can take for those things to get through customs, and then yell at you every single day for the two months it takes for the package to clear customs in the other country and finally get returned to our offices.

E-mail
(Overenthusiastic Monitoring of)

If you actually do get to go on a business trip with me, I will not make you spend the entire time there at the hotel's business center, constantly refreshing my e-mail so I don't miss a single thing, even though we're in a different time zone, and our business is closed during most of the time we're awake.

Time Zones *(Abusing)*

If you are in our offices in London and I am on a business trip to New York, I will not make you stay in the office until 10 P.M. "just in case someone important calls."

Airline Miles
(Pointless Collection of)

I will not make you spend hours on the phone with different airline customer service representatives, trying to get them to give me reward miles on trips I took two years ago—reward miles that I will never have the inclination or need to use, since I'm rich enough to buy myself business-class tickets with pound sterling.

Presents *(Exclusions)*

When I return from a holiday bearing fun gifts for everyone in the office, I will bring one for you, too. I will not leave you out and then, when called out on it by a colleague, try to explain by saying, "Oh, I buy him/her stuff like this all the time," a transparently false statement that I make with zero shame.

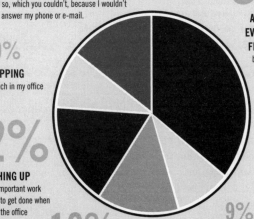

15%
FRANTICALLY HANDLING ALL THE WORK EMERGENCIES
that I forgot to deal with before I left, even though you reminded me to do so five times a day for a full week, and then later listening to me yell at you for not consulting me before you did so, which you couldn't, because I wouldn't answer my phone or e-mail.

9%
NAPPING
on the couch in my office

22%
CATCHING UP
on all the important work you're unable to get done when I'm at the office

10%
AWKWARDLY READING A LANGUAGE
you don't speak from Google Translate over the phone to a bemused waiter

35%
ASSURING ME THAT EVERYTHING IS GOING FINE AT THE OFFICE,
because there is nothing happening at the office to go wrong

9%
BOOKING RESTAURANT RESERVATIONS FOR ME,
and then canceling them when I decide to just order room service

WHAT YOU'LL BE DOING WHILE I'M ON HOLIDAY
A Breakdown

14%

SIGHTSEEING AND TAKING A SERIES OF TERRIBLE SNAPSHOTS

with a digital camera that cost more than you make in two months, which I will then make you spend hours editing in Photoshop, so that I can upload the best ones to a Facebook album casually titled, "just a few pix from my vacay LOL"

20%

CATCHING UP

on all the sleep I've missed since my last vacation two years ago

16%

ROLLING CALLS POOLSIDE,

because I don't actually know how to relax anymore

10%

COMPLAINING

about the service/food/bedding/light-bulbs/carpets/price of everything at my five-star hotel

31%

COMPULSIVELY CHECKING MY BLACKBERRY

for e-mails every five minutes, while trying to hide it from my significant other

9%

DRINKING AND EATING

all the things I don't allow myself at home

WHAT I'LL BE DOING WHILE I'M ON HOLIDAY
A Breakdown

IMs FROM HELL: **BOOKING FLIGHTS**
(Importance of Paying Attention to Details)

BOSS: these flight times you sent me are no good

11:16 A.M.

ASSISTANT: I'm sorry—should I look at a different airline? Is there an exact time you'd like to leave?

11:17 A.M.

BOSS: no. american airlines. and not these times.

11:18 A.M.

ASSISTANT: Unfortunately these are the only nonstop flights on this date available on American.

11:26 A.M.

BOSS: i just looked online and there are 3 more flights on this day that u didnt send me!!!11!!

11:26 A.M.

BOSS: 10:07a, 12:40p, 3:06p

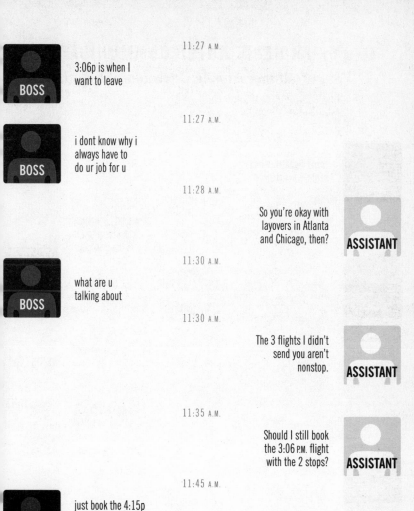

11:27 A.M.

BOSS: 3:06p is when I want to leave

11:27 A.M.

BOSS: i dont know why i always have to do ur job for u

11:28 A.M.

ASSISTANT: So you're okay with layovers in Atlanta and Chicago, then?

11:30 A.M.

BOSS: what are u talking about

11:30 A.M.

ASSISTANT: The 3 flights I didn't send you aren't nonstop.

11:35 A.M.

ASSISTANT: Should I still book the 3:06 P.M. flight with the 2 stops?

11:45 A.M.

BOSS: just book the 4:15p nonstop and quit bothering me about it

IMs FROM HELL: **HOTEL COMMUNICATION**
(Unnecessarily Convoluted)

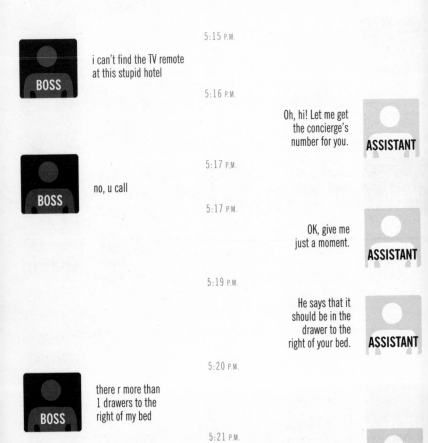

5:15 P.M.

BOSS
i can't find the TV remote at this stupid hotel

5:16 P.M.

Oh, hi! Let me get the concierge's number for you.
ASSISTANT

5:17 P.M.

BOSS
no, u call

5:17 P.M.

OK, give me just a moment.
ASSISTANT

5:19 P.M.

He says that it should be in the drawer to the right of your bed.
ASSISTANT

5:20 P.M.

BOSS
there r more than 1 drawers to the right of my bed

5:21 P.M.

One moment.
ASSISTANT

5:23 P.M.

It should be in the top
drawer of the small
table directly to the
right of your bed. **ASSISTANT**

5:24 P.M.

Do you see it? **ASSISTANT**

5:35 P.M.

Hello? **ASSISTANT**

6:15 P.M.

BOSS can u pls find out
where the room
service menu is?

6:15 P.M.

Sure. **ASSISTANT**

6:15 P.M.

Just a moment. **ASSISTANT**

NAVIGATION

If I Ever Make It to an Outside Meeting on Time,

It's by Accident

Navigation Devices

(Choosing One, Not All)

I will not demand that you print out a Google map for me every time I leave the office and put the address of my destination into my GPS, and then, once I'm in the car, ignore both of those helpful things and have you navigate the route for me over the phone.

GPS *(Necessity of)*

I will have one in my car. There is absolutely no reason for me not to have one, especially if, having spent my whole life in the city we live in, I still get lost in the streets surrounding our offices.

Errands *(Unknown)*

I will not come into the office at 10:30 A.M. "pissed off" because you didn't make me a map for the errand you didn't know I was running that morning.

My Navigational Abilities

(Overestimation of)

When you're driving me somewhere neither of us has ever been before, I will not insist that "we don't need that thing" (referring to your handy GPS), get us very lost in a terrible part of town, and then explain that "your bad driving confused me."

Taking Offense
(Unnecessarily)

If I have a tendency to get lost, and I know that I do, and you know that I do, I will be grateful, not insulted, when you print me a map for even my most basic trips or nag me repeatedly to leave just a little bit early for an important meeting.

Impressive Navigation
(from a Distance)

When I'm traveling in another city, I will not call you from my rental car, screaming about how lost I am, give you the name of the last street sign I saw, expect you to figure out exactly where I am, and then hang up on you without a word of thanks when you actually manage to do so.

Directions to My House
(Failures)

When you have to go over to my house for the first time ever to water my plants while I'm out of town, I will not forget to mention that the street my house is on has no street signs and is very difficult to see from the main road, and that all Internet map generators and GPS devices tend to provide incorrect directions to it.

Directional Questions
(Unnecessary)

When you're giving me directions over the phone as I'm driving to a meeting, and you tell me to turn left on a certain street, I will not ask, "My left or your left?" and then get mad at you when I miss the turn while you try to explain (unsuccessfully) that they are one and the same.

Human Error *(Results of)*

I will not enter the wrong street number into my car's GPS and blame you when the location of my meeting turns out to be two miles away from where I parked.

Clarity *(Extra-Special)*

I will not ask you to print me a map to the restaurant where I'm having lunch, even though it is across the street from our offices, and then blame you for "not making it clear enough" when I still manage to get lost.

GPS Devices *(Importance of Correct Settings)*

I will not insist that my GPS is "broken" and make you drive over to my house to take a look at it, only for you to discover that I've set it up to automatically choose a country that is one thousand miles away from the one we actually live in.

Shortcuts *(Opposite of)*

When you're driving me somewhere, I will not insist that you take "my secret shortcut," which, rather than making our journey shorter, instead forces you to spend an extra twenty minutes in the car with me due to the traffic on the route that I still insist is "way better than yours."

Post Codes *(Importance of)*

When there are two streets in our city with similar names, I will not confirm that I mean to go to an address on one street, and then blame you when it turns out that I actually wanted to go to the other one.

iPhone Maps *(Data Usage of)*

When out of the country, I will not fail to tell you that I'm using my iPhone as a navigational device instead of the maps you made me, and then act shocked when I get the bill for all the data I used internationally, which you would have warned me about had you known.

Directions *(Impossibly Specific)*

When you hand me a map showing how to get from my office to a meeting at another office, I will not ask you why there are no directions for inside the actual building, as if you have not made me hundreds of maps before, all of which directed me to the building entrance and trusted that I had enough common sense to find my way from there.

Remote Viewing *(Impossibility of)*

After talking on the phone with someone for thirty minutes while driving to a place I've never been before, I will not hang up, call you and ask, "Where am I?" and expect an accurate answer immediately. I will acknowledge that you are not able to track my real-time location from your desk.

GPS Devices *(Vital Functions of)*

When you finally convince me to get a GPS for my car, help me pick out the best and most well-reviewed model, and set it up so that not even my toddler could screw it up, I will not call you from my car to say that I'm completely lost, because "that thing's voice was annoying me, so I turned it off."

New York City *(Unfounded Claims About)*

While on a business trip to New York City, I will not insist that you "just provide me with the cross streets of places—I know this city like the back of my hand," and then blame you when I spend most of my time there completely lost, as it turns out that I don't know the back of my hand at all.

Rental Car GPS *(Low Cost of Having, High Cost of Not Having)*

I will spring for the extra £12 a day it costs for me to get a GPS in my rental car when I'm on a business trip to a city I've never been to before, instead of having you e-mail me directions to and from everywhere I want to go and then blaming you when I miss a turn and end up in a nasty part of town.

Alternate Routes *(Terrible Suggestions)*

I will not suggest a new route for you to take to work, insisting that "it will cut your commute in half—you'll be thanking me tomorrow," and then yell at you when you show up to work twenty minutes late the next day, having given my suggestion a try. (You really should have known better, though.)

Finding Me *(Inventive Solutions That Really Shouldn't Be Necessary)*

I will not get so lost in the city I've lived in for the past twenty years that you have to resort to turning on the "find my iPhone" function on my mobile phone to figure out where I am and how I can get to where I'm supposed to be going.

Directions *(Very Basic Terminology)*

When you're giving me directions over the phone and use simple words like *north, south, east,* and *west* to try to point me the right way, I will not complain that I "don't know what that means."

Landmarks *(Unhelpful)*

When I'm lost, and you ask me if I see any street signs, addresses, or landmarks that might help you to figure out where I am, I will not name things such as "McDonald's," "Starbucks," "the number seven in the address but I couldn't see the other numbers," or "that bar I went to for drinks once but didn't like."

Distractions *(Requested)*

I will not blame you for distracting me and causing me to miss a motorway exit by five miles, when you were just transferring calls to my mobile phone, which is exactly what I asked you to do.

Preparation *(Pointless)*

I will not insist that you give me printed-out maps for my trips an hour before I leave so I can look them over, but then, once I've looked them over, absentmindedly put them in a stack of papers on my desk and forget to take them with me in the car.

Running on Autopilot *(Then Blaming It on You)*

I will not zone out while driving to a dinner meeting, find myself pulling up to my own house instead of the restaurant, and then, too embarrassed to reveal what I've done to you or the person I'm now late to meet with, convince you that you gave me directions to the wrong restaurant, forcing you to apologize to me and the person I'm meeting with and then spend the rest of the night wondering if you're going crazy.

Traffic Tickets *(Attempts to Deflect the Cost of)*

When I get a ticket for driving the wrong way down a one-way street, I will not try to convince you that you should pay for it, "since you're the one who gave me directions," which I obviously did not follow.

Punctuality *(Apparently a Terrible Thing)*

I will not get mad at you when you perfectly estimate the amount of time it will take me to get from our offices to an outside meeting, so that I arrive exactly five minutes early, which I later insist "made me look like an overeager junior executive!!!"

Following Me While Driving *(Possibly to Your Death)*

If I can't remember the address, name, or cross streets of a place we both have to travel to in our cars, I will not suggest that "you can just follow me there," and then lead you on what is basically a high-speed chase throughout the city, forcing you to run numerous red lights and cut off more than one person, and then, when we finally reach our destination and park, get out of my car, and, upon seeing your white face and knuckles, exclaim, "Oh! I totally forgot you were following me here!"

Navigational Systems *(New and Complicated Versus Old and Simple)*

When I get a brand-new smartphone, I will not wave away the printed-out maps you try to hand me, insisting that "I don't need those anymore," and then, fifteen minutes later, call you from my brand-new smartphone to complain that "I don't know how this thing works" and ask for step-by-step directions to where I need to go.

THE MAP YOU MADE ME FOR MY BUSINESS TRIP

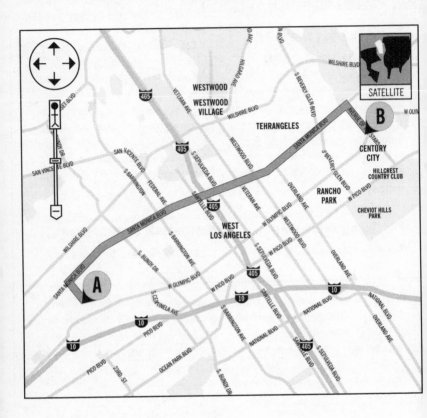

HOW I INTERPRETED IT, MAKING MYSELF TWENTY MINUTES LATE FOR A MEETING, WHICH I BLAMED ON YOU

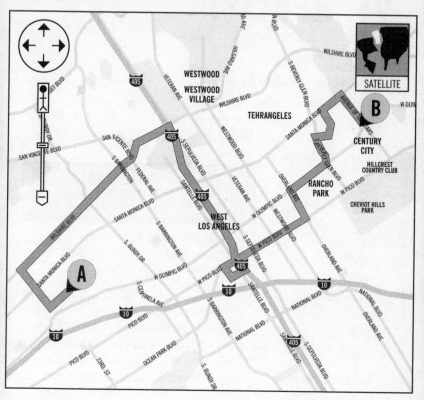

EXPECTATION VS. REALITY

How I Follow Instructions (After Accusing You of Not Being Able to Do So at Least Once a Day)

DIRECTIONS MY GPS GIVES ME	HOW I ACT ON THEM
"Turn right."	Come to a complete stop in the right lane for a full minute as I try to figure out if the street I'm supposed to turn right on is this one or the next one.
"Turn left."	Veer suddenly across three lanes of traffic to make it into a left-turn lane before realizing that the next street is the one I'm supposed to turn onto.
"Continue on this street for the next 2.5 miles."	Zone out, find myself on a motorway entrance ramp that "just came out of nowhere" and is now taking me in the opposite direction of where I need to go.
"Turn around when possible."	Make a wildly unsafe illegal U-turn, and then later tell you that "this thing almost killed me" while waving the GPS in your face, as if it's all your fault.
"You have reached your destination."	Continue driving for at least another half-mile, until the GPS tells me to "turn around when possible."

14%

I GAVE YOU THE WRONG ADDRESS
and insisted it was the right one even when you double-checked with me

26%

I DIDN'T PAY ATTENTION
to you when you were explaining a confusing part of the route

10%

I REFUSED A MAP YOU OFFERED ME,
insisting that I knew where I was going

18%

I GOT DISTRACTED WHILE GOSSIPING
with a colleague on the phone and made five wrong turns

11%

I HAVE A MAP, A GPS, AND YOU ON THE PHONE READING ME DIRECTIONS,
but I'm just a terrible driver, and that's that

21%

I LEFT THE DETAILED MAP
you printed for me on my desk

REASONS WHY I'M LOST
A Breakdown

TRANSPORTATION

From Point A to Point B, Painfully

Driving Together, Part 1

If you are unlucky enough to have to drive me somewhere, I will not say "Oops!" and shoot you a reproachful look from the passenger seat every time we drive over railroad tracks or an uneven section of the road, as if the bumpy ride is all your fault.

Driving Together, Part 2

When you're behind the wheel, and we're sitting at a red light, I will not lean ever-so-slightly forward in my seat so that I can see the light and bark "Green!" the millisecond it changes, continuing my favorite hobby of making sure you always look like you weren't paying attention.

Driving Together, Part 3

When you're driving me somewhere, I won't slam on the imaginary brakes on the passenger side of the car every five minutes because I inexplicably think you're going to hit someone.

Driving Together, Part 4

As soon as I get into your car so you can drive me somewhere, I will not turn the air-conditioning up to full blast and insist that we leave it that way for the entire thirty-minute trip, so that you end up feeling like you're going to freeze to death in your own car by the time we arrive.

Shame (Feeling Some but Not Enough)

I will not make you drive me to a doctor's appointment and insist that you "just hang out in your car" while I'm there, because I'm embarrassed that I'm making you act as my chauffeur (but not embarrassed enough to stop doing it).

Mileage (Approval of)

When you hand me your mileage sheet to approve for reimbursement, I will not cross out all the miles you drove for my own personal errands, explain that "accounting won't let this kind of thing slide," and not even offer to give you the petrol money out of my own pocket.

Money (Carrying)

I will carry change in my car, pockets, or purse for parking. I will not call you frantically from an appointment with my fancy dermatologist to make you drive five miles in traffic to fill up my parking meter for me, with your own money.

My Car (Buying)

I will not make you negotiate the price for the expensive new car I want to buy and then scream obscenities at you and insult all of your abilities as an assistant because you only got within £200 of what I wanted to pay.

Your Car (Borrowing)

If I'm without a car for the day, I will not ask to borrow yours for an hour or so, and then return it with the tank empty, the petrol light on, and not a word about reimbursing you for the inexplicably large amounts of fuel I managed to use up in so short a time.

Your Car (Not-So-Subtle Insults)

I will not ask to borrow your car for the day while mine is in the shop, and then, upon seeing that it's clean, well kept, but also a ten-year-old Honda Civic, put the keys back into your hand and say, "On second thought, a taxi won't be that expensive."

Demands *(Adding Salt to Your Wounds)*

When you're in a car accident and forced to take the bus to work for a week because you can't afford a rental car, I will not make your life even worse by demanding that you still stop by my favorite juice place every day to pick up a smoothie for me, which now tacks an extra hour onto your already painful commute.

How to Burn Out Your Clutch *(in Just One Week!)*

I will not insist that you teach my teenaged child how to drive in your own car.

Skills *(Time-Saving but Not Allowed)*

When my car's battery dies in the office garage, I will not refuse your offers to jump-start it, saying that "we don't need you blowing anything up today," and instead force you to spend your lunch hour waiting for the AA to come and do something you could've done in five minutes.

Fuel *(Something I Am Capable of Buying Myself)*

I will not make you go fill my car up with petrol during your lunch hour because I think I'm too important to do so myself on my way to or from work.

Children *(Effects on the Interiors of Cars)*

If part of your job description is driving my children to and from school and/or extracurricular activities, I will pay for your car to be cleaned on a regular basis instead of making fun of you for all the food, drink, mud, and grubby fingerprints that are now a pretty much constant presence inside your car.

Convenience
(Being Ridiculous About)

I will not expect you to keep spare sets of the keys to my four luxury cars (which, combined on one key chain, weigh about one pound and are the size of a toddler's head) and be available at all times to bring them to me when I can't find my keys, which is all the time, due to the fact that I don't have the attention span to look for them for more than thirty seconds without getting distracted by something else.

Washing My Car *(Ambushes)*

I will not ask you to take my car to a specific car wash, only for you to find out upon your arrival that it's one of those wash-it-yourself places, and that I expect you to do so, causing you to splash water all over yourself and turn the rest of the workday into a one-person wet-T-shirt contest, all so I can save a few pounds.

Suggestions *(Impossible)*

After I buy my kid a BMW for his sixteenth birthday, I will not go on at length about what a great car it is and how you should totally get one, too, and then act offended when you reply that you'd love to but you just can't afford it, asking if you "think my kid is a spoiled brat or something!?"

Your Driving Skills
(Condescension Toward)

When I need you to drive my car somewhere for me, I will not first insist that you drive it around the block with me in the passenger seat, "just to make sure you can handle it," even though I've had more car accidents in the past year than you've had in your entire life.

Illegal Parking
(Awareness of)

When I'm running late to a meeting, I will not park my car in the loading zone behind our office, fail to let you know that I've done so, and then blame you when I get a parking ticket and threaten to take it out of your wages.

Parking Tickets
(Failed Predictions of)

I will not have you park your car in a non-parking space when you're driving me somewhere, insisting that "there's no way you'll get a ticket—we'll only be five minutes!" and then not even offer to pay for it when you do in fact get a parking ticket that costs close to the amount of money you make in a day.

Scratches *(Mysterious Appearances of)*

I will not borrow your car for an hour and return it with a giant scratch on its bumper, insisting that "it was there before" (it wasn't).

Principles *(Confusing)*

I will not make you drive fifteen miles round-trip on your lunch break (the only hour of almost happiness in your entire day) to fill up my car at the station with the lowest petrol prices in the city, insisting that it's worth it "as a matter of principle" even though you've calculated that it will save me £3 total, and the petrol station is actually on my way home from work.

Sensible Cars
(Different Opinions About)

If I ask you to put together a list of "nice, sensible cars that aren't ostentatious" for me to buy to replace my two-year-old luxury car, and you give me a list that includes cars like the Prius, but nothing along the lines of Mercedes or BMW, I will not crumple it into a ball with the words "This was supposed to be a list of cars for me, not for you," and eventually just end up leasing a brand-new BMW SUV.

Maintenance Skills
(Appreciation of)

When you offer to jump-start my car or change a flat tire for me, I will respond with sincere thanks that you're saving me time and money, instead of suspicion that you plan to sabotage my car.

Bluetooth Systems *(Canceling Out the Efficiency of)*

If I have a Bluetooth system in my car that connects my mobile phone to the car's speakers, so I can make calls without using a headset, I will take the time to learn how to use it correctly, instead of relying on you to walk down to the garage with me every time I leave the office to set it up, which, depending on how many meetings I have, could be as many as six times on any given day, or almost a full hour of walking to and from the garage to do something an eight-year-old could learn to do in fifteen minutes.

Suggestions *(Inconsiderate)*

After catching a glimpse of your old but functional car, I will not suggest that you look into getting a new one, because "appearance is everything in this town, and a little investment in the way you present yourself to people goes a long way," conveniently ignoring the fact that I don't pay you enough for you to invest in a new bicycle, let alone a car.

Accidents *(Wrong Place, Wrong Time, Wrong Boss)*

When you are rear-ended by someone with no insurance while on a personal errand for me, I will offer to help you pay to get your car repaired, rather than saying only, "That sucks. Did you get [the thing I asked you to pick up for me]?"

Justifications *(Transparent)*

I will not buy my sixteen-year-old child a car that costs double your annual salary and insist that "my kid isn't spoiled—it's because of safety."

Blame *(Nice Try)*

I will not accuse you of scratching my car when you returned it to the garage after refueling it, only rescinding my accusation when you suggest that we take a look at the security tapes for the day, since I know that they will show me, not you, scraping the side of my car against a concrete pillar.

Parking *(Resentful Reimbursement for)*

When you have to run an errand that involves parking at a paid lot, I will pay you back for the parking, even if it's only £3, rather than accusing you of being "cheap" when you have to ask me to do so, and then tossing the money at you while you're sitting at your desk, so you have to pick it up off the floor in front of the entire office.

Transportation Situations *(Completely Unpredictable)*

When the driver of a perfectly reputable car service gets pulled over by the police while taking me home from the airport and ends up being arrested for failure to pay his child support, causing me to have to catch a taxi for the rest of the trip, I will not call you on the ride and yell at you for not booking the car service through a "less sketchy" company, even though we've always used this one, have never had a problem with them before, and I told you specifically to book me the same driver I had for my last trip.

Cabbies *(Are People, Too)*

I will not call you from the cab you sent to pick me up at a bar after I got too drunk to drive to ask "why you picked out a weird cabbie," as if you had any choice over the matter and the cabdriver can't hear anything I'm saying.

New Cars
(Apparent Implications of)

When you've finally saved up enough money to replace your fifteen-year-old clunker with a brand-new car, I will not snidely suggest that it's a sign I'm paying you too much, even though I've been saying since the first week you started working for me that "you really should get a better car."

School Pride *(Ridiculing)*

When I see that you have a sticker with the name of your university on the back of your non-luxury vehicle, I will not point to it, snort, and say, "A lot of good those three years did you."

Hellos *(Dangerously Out of Character)*

If I see you driving your car on a weekend, I will not try to pull up beside you and get your attention by honking my horn, yelling out my window, and swerving dangerously close to you, all so I can surprise you and say hi, something I would try to avoid doing if I ran into you while walking on the street.

Big Cars *(the Point of)*

I will not make you try to fit the small-but-not-that-small bookshelf I need taken over to my house inside your tiny economy car, when it would clearly fit quite easily into the trunk of my excessively large SUV, but for the fact that "I don't want to damage the upholstery."

Terrible Drivers *(Feeling Like One Versus Just Being One)*

When driving both of us somewhere, I will not turn corners with such violence that you're forced to grab the handle on the ceiling of the car to stop yourself from crashing into the window or falling onto my lap, and then, once we're traveling in a straight line again, ask you if "you're trying to make me feel like a bad driver or something."

Sunglasses

(Necessity Versus Luxury)

When you're driving me some-where in the middle of the day, and I leave my sunglasses at the office, I will not ask to borrow yours in a tone that says you can't refuse, so that you're forced to squint painfully as you drive toward the sun, while I relax in my seat and enjoy the ride, occa-sionally suggesting that you "step on it a little and stop driving like my grandmother."

Making Enemies *(on Your Behalf)*

When you're driving me some-where and someone cuts you off, I will not consider it my responsibility to flip that driver the bird and yell obscenities out the window, even though it's pretty clear the driver is some-one's very old, very oblivious grandmother.

Safe Driving (Always Trumps Punctuality, No Matter What I Think)

I will not call you on your mobile phone when I know you're on your way to the office, forcing you to pull over to answer it safely, spend a good twenty minutes rattling off a list of things I need you to do that I didn't have the patience to type into an e-mail, so that you have to write them all down in order to remember them later, and then get mad at you when you're fifteen minutes late to work, insisting that you should be "equipped" to answer my calls at any time of day, which apparently means your "equipment" should be a self-driving car.

Spare Tires (Forgetfulness)

I will not ask you to meet me ten miles away from the office so you can help me change my tire, because my AA membership is expired (something I will try to blame on you), only for you to arrive and find an empty space in my trunk where the spare tire should be, because I got a flat last year and forgot to replace it, and then make you put your own spare tire on my car rather than waiting twenty minutes for someone from my dealership to bring one to me, "because I have to get to the office for that important meeting" (which you know is a lie due to the fact that you know my calendar better than I do).

Drinking (Facing the Consequences of Like a Grown-up)

When I leave my car outside a bar because I was too drunk to drive home, and the car gets towed and sent to a lot some twenty miles outside the city, I will take a cab there and pick it up myself, instead of calling you first thing on Sunday morning and asking you to "find a friend" to help you do it for me.

Taxis (Single-Occupancy Only, Apparently)

I will not flat-out refuse to share a cab with you, offering you no excuses except for the word *no*, even though we're both traveling to the same place, from the office, at the same time.

WHAT MY CAR SAYS ABOUT ME

(It's a Lot More Than You'd Think)

MY CAR	ME
Luxury SUV	I just want to fit in with all of my other rich and boring friends who own cars that are different brands and colors than mine, but are almost indistinguishable from each other in terms of shape.
Prius	I am either a completely down-to-earth, responsible, environmentally conscious person, or, more likely, I just want people to think I am.
Ostentatious sports car	All I want in life is for people to think I'm awesome all the time, even when I'm just driving to work.

MY CAR	ME
Hummer or some other behemoth that guzzles the equivalent of the GDP of a small country in gas every year	I may be living out my life as a rich executive, but inside, I think I deserve to be a reality TV star.
Luxury estate	I have kids, but still try to assert my status as an Important Hip Person through the brand name of my car, even though no one ever looked at a BMW estate and thought, "Wow—cool car," a fact that I am subconsciously aware of but will never admit to myself, further adding to my resentment of my children for ruining my life.
The cheapest model of a luxury brand	I care entirely about appearances, not quality; otherwise I'd have a much cheaper car that would end up lasting me twice as long.
A normal car that normal people drive	I am a normal person. Just kidding! I owe massive debts to someone from my past who would come after me if he or she ever found out I spent more than I needed to on a car. Otherwise, I'd totally have one of the other kind.

11%

HELPING ME SEARCH FOR MY KEYS, which will usually end up being at the bottom of my bag, or in my pocket

4%

LOOKING FOR ITS REPLACEMENT EVERY 8 MONTHS or so, whenever one of my colleagues buys a newer model

48%

DRIVING IT TO AND FROM the mechanic's, the petrol station, or the car wash, while worrying that you're going to crash it

11%

LISTENING TO ME BRAG about how great it is

11%

LISTENING TO ME COMPLAIN about how terrible it is

15%

DRIVING ME SOMEWHERE IN IT, listening to me brag about how great it is

YOUR INTERACTIONS WITH MY CAR
A Breakdown

5

MAKING *things* PERSONAL

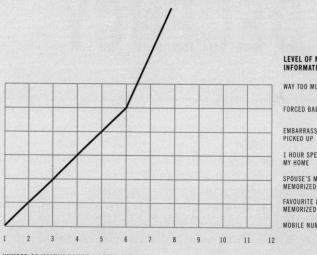

LEVEL OF MY PERSONAL INFORMATION KNOWN

WAY TOO MUCH

FORCED BABYSITTING

EMBARRASSING PRESCRIPTIONS PICKED UP

1 HOUR SPENT INSIDE MY HOME

SPOUSE'S MOBILE NUMBER MEMORIZED

FAVOURITE LUNCH ORDERS MEMORIZED

MOBILE NUMBER MEMORIZED

1 2 3 4 5 6 7 8 9 10 11 12

NUMBER OF MONTHS YOU'VE WORKED FOR ME

BASIC HUMAN DECENCY

Not Ruining Your Entire Life, Just Parts of It

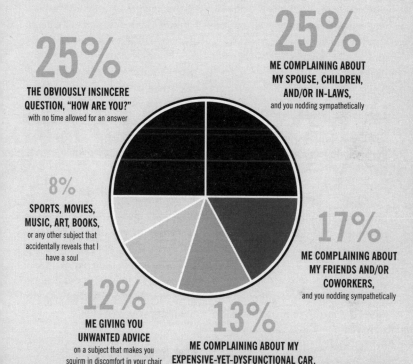

25%

THE OBVIOUSLY INSINCERE
QUESTION, "HOW ARE YOU?"
with no time allowed for an answer

25%

ME COMPLAINING ABOUT
MY SPOUSE, CHILDREN,
AND/OR IN-LAWS,
and you nodding sympathetically

8%

SPORTS, MOVIES,
MUSIC, ART, BOOKS,
or any other subject that
accidentally reveals that I
have a soul

17%

ME COMPLAINING ABOUT
MY FRIENDS AND/OR
COWORKERS,
and you nodding sympathetically

12%

ME GIVING YOU
UNWANTED ADVICE
on a subject that makes you
squirm in discomfort in your chair

13%

ME COMPLAINING ABOUT MY
EXPENSIVE-YET-DYSFUNCTIONAL CAR,
and you nodding sympathetically

CONVERSATIONS WE HAVE THAT AREN'T ABOUT WORK
A Breakdown

Bitterness *(Cause and Effect)*

I will not call you into my office, ask you to shut the door, and explain that I'm going to replace you with someone who is "more enthusiastic about the business, you know, less jaded," when the reason you've become so jaded is that you've worked for me for the past two years.

Exclusion *(Retaliatory)*

I will not laugh and joke around with other assistants during our weekly staff meeting but, as soon as you open your mouth to join in, fix you with a cold glare of pure disdain, all because you put too much Splenda in my coffee that morning.

Betrayals *(Loud)*

After we agree that our working together is beneficial to neither of us, and I then overhear you explaining to the company's CFO that you will be applying for the dole upon your departure, I will not exclaim, "The dole! You quit on me!" for all the office to hear.

Mentorship *(Providing)*

If, after a year of busting your ass as my assistant, you ask if I have a few minutes to discuss the possibility of your career advancing at the company and any advice I might have for you, I will not reply by rolling my eyes and saying, "I don't have time for that. You'll figure it out yourself, just like I had to," even though it is widely known around the business that my first boss was a very supportive mentor and had a great impact on my own success.

Efficiency *(Incentives)*

When you manage to increase the efficiency of my office and actually do all the tasks I've given you in a reasonable time period, I will not reward you by decreasing your hours, thereby significantly reducing your paycheck.

Your Replacement
(Premeditation)

I will not start advertising for your replacement before telling you that I'm replacing you. If things are that bad, I should realize that you're probably already looking at all the job postings and will recognize your own job immediately.

Your Future
(Catching a Glimpse of)

When I tell you to reschedule a certain lunch for the fifth time in two months, I will not try to explain myself by telling you, "[So-and-So] used to be my assistant, so it's not really that important."

Considerate Questions *(Fake)*

I will not ask if you have any plans on a Friday night and, when you say you're actually having dinner with an old friend you haven't seen in a while, say, "That's too bad. I need you to stay late."

Birthdays *(Yours)*

If I never made an effort to figure out your birthday, I won't get mad at you for "making me look like an asshole" when I come in to work and find you sitting happily at your desk surrounded by presents and cards from people who actually care about you.

Personal Space *(Respecting Yours)*

I won't walk up behind you as you're hard at work at your desk and start picking hairs off your back as if we're monkeys.

Compliments *(Backhanded)*

I will never ask if you "made your earrings yourself," especially if you have never indicated to me that jewelry making is among your hobbies.

Your Name *(Spelling It)*

When your name can be spelled a number of ways, or has an unusual spelling, or neither, I will take the time to spell it correctly, rather than consistently misspelling it in my e-mails, despite the fact that I have to spell it correctly every time I type your e-mail address, thereby causing my colleagues to frequently reply to my e-mails with the question "Who's [your name, misspelled beyond recognition]?"

The Thermostat
(Use as a Torture Device)

I will keep our office at a temperature that allows you to be comfortable in your regular clothes, not at temperatures that force you to bring a heavy coat to work during the summer and strip down to your undershirt during winter.

Knowledge *(Yours)*

I will never sneeringly call you a "nerd," "geek," "smart-arse," "dweeb," "overachieving freak," or "weirdo" just because you know more than I do about a specific subject that I asked you for information about.

Introductions *(Inclusion of Unnecessary Information)*

After I introduce you with the normal niceties to a colleague who's visiting our office for the first time, I will not then say, as a point of interest about you, "[Assistant] has lost a lot of weight since [he or she] first started working for me," and then smile proudly, as if I had something to do with it.

Personal Possessions
(What's Yours Is Mine)

When talking to a colleague near your desk, I will not absentmindedly grab your lip balm, use it, and then put it back, no permission asked or thanks given.

Overtime *(Caps)*

If our company has a cap on assistants' overtime hours, I will not make you work more than you're allowed to put on your time sheet. If extenuating circumstances require you to do so, I will pay you in cash. I will not, however, insist that you work eleven-hour days, not offer to compensate you for the hours of your life that I'm stealing from you, and then, to top it all off, give you a terrible holiday bonus.

Compliments
(Wrong Way to Accept)

If you ever compliment me on an item of clothing and ask where I got it, I will accept the compliment graciously and tell you the name of the store, rather than saying, apologetically, "It's really expensive."

Incentives (Incorrect)

I will not bring up the amount of money I'm paying you every time I feel like you're not working hard enough, causing you to feel guilty about a paycheck that is barely enough for you to live on.

Sympathy (Problems Deserving of)

I will not refuse to have any sympathy for you when you get a speeding ticket, caused by my asking you to get to work thirty minutes early with barely any notice, but expect you to coo over me when I complain that there was too much lemon juice in my smoothie that morning.

Gloating (Belittling)

I will not frequently tell you that "you don't even know how many people want to work with me," implying that you should therefore feel lucky that you have the opportunity to be treated badly by me.

Preemptive Strikes (Slander)

If I run into you at a bar on a weekend and see you actually having fun and relaxing with a group of friends, I will greet you politely and move on. I will not, however, come in to work on Monday crowing about how drunk you were, when it was actually I who was the drunk one, and I just want to make sure that your credibility is torn down before you can tell anyone about the impressive face plant I did on the dance floor.

Obvious Changes (Noticing)

When you dramatically change your hairstyle, I will say, "Nice haircut," instead of saying absolutely nothing and therefore making you feel more invisible than you already did.

One-Time Deals
(Taking Advantage of)

I will not take your willingness to stay up until midnight one time to help me with a project as an indication that you're willing to stay up working every night until midnight, and then accuse you of having a terrible work ethic when you let me know that isn't the case.

Your Special Day (Sugarless)

When it's company tradition for bosses to buy their assistants a cake or cupcakes for their birthday, I will not be the only boss in the office who forgets to do so, even though all the other assistants have been sending me reminder e-mails every day the week leading up to it.

Phone Chargers (Cost of)

I will not steal your iPhone charger and iPhone earbuds so frequently (always denying that I've done so) that by the end of the year you've spent almost a full paycheck replacing them.

Decoration (Cruel Destruction of)

I will not knock your favorite plant (the one cheerful sign of life that will fit in your cubicle) off your desk and tell you to clean up the mess before someone steps in it, without even offering to replace it.

Eye Contact (Basic Rules of)

When having a conversation with you, I will look you in the eye. I will not, however, look down at whatever papers are in my hand when you speak, as if your half of the conversation isn't important at all, nor will I look at a point in space slightly above your left ear, as if I can't bear to look at your face.

Imitations (Uncalled for)

I will not suddenly adopt a cartoonishly unhelpful and whiny attitude when you ask me a routine question and then, upon seeing the confused look on your face, explain, "That's how it is for me when I talk to you."

Rubbish *(as Torture Device)*

I will not make you go out back and dig through the office's rubbish bin to find something that I think I accidentally threw away, which I will later find at the bottom of one of my desk drawers.

Jokes *(Revealing)*

After the CEO of the company gives a speech at the office holiday party, thanking all of the assistants and support staff, and everyone applauds, I will not "jokingly" shout out, "Except for [your name]!"

Fake-outs *(Doubly Cruel)*

I will not hand you a shopping bag from an expensive store, saying, "Here, these are for you," only for you to excitedly open it to find a tangle of all your cell phone chargers that I've borrowed over the past year, some of which have been chewed through by my dog.

Paranoia *(Causing)*

I will not suddenly stop talking whenever you enter a room I'm in, giving you the sneaking suspicion that, every time I'm out of your earshot, I'm complaining about you.

Playing Favorites *(Against You)*

I will not throw you under the bus during a staff meeting, not to cover up for one of my mistakes but to cover up for someone else's assistant, because I think that assistant has a bright future at the company and you don't.

Communication Middlemen *(Really Annoying)*

When I get a new puppy and bring it to the office, I won't spend an entire day only speaking to you in baby talk through the "voice" of the puppy.

Encouragements *(Embarrassing)*

When I need you to get up from a staff meeting and retrieve something from your desk for me, I will ask you in a whisper or discreetly pass you a note. I will not clap my hands and yell, "Run, run, run!" making you actually do so in front of the entire company.

Moods (Extreme)

If I have only two distinct moods at my disposal—one where I try to act like a cool boss and be your best friend, and the other where I snap at the slightest mistake or imagined hint of disrespect—I will not flip back and forth between them with absolutely no warning.

Guilt (Correct Reaction to)

If I yell at you for something and then later realize that it wasn't your fault, I will apologize to you instead of silently resenting you for the rest of the week for making me experience the unfamiliar feeling of guilt.

Humiliation (Setting You Up for)

I will not let you go into your first-ever company presentation with a big piece of spinach stuck between your teeth and then make fun of you about it later.

Hopes (Dashed)

As we're packing up and getting ready to leave for the night, I will not ask, "Oh, did you [do a completely unimportant thing that I never asked you to do, which will take at least two hours]?" and then demand that you do it at once.

Guessing Games (Condescending)

When you give me a document to make notes on, I will tell you what I want you to change, rather than walking out to your desk, pointing to a paragraph, and asking, "What do you think is wrong with this?" making you guess over and over again until I finally reveal that you used the same word twice in one sentence.

Welcoming Parties (Terrible)

I will not welcome you back from surgery with a lecture about how the temp did a much better job than you ever have, and then whine about the fact that you're on crutches and therefore can't bring me coffee for the next six weeks.

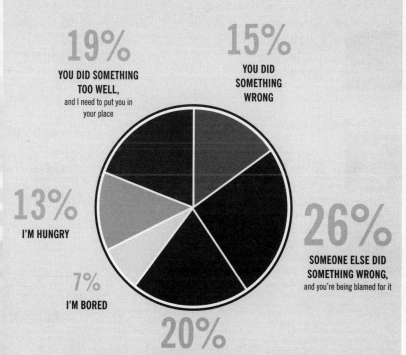

19%
YOU DID SOMETHING
TOO WELL,
and I need to put you in
your place

15%
YOU DID
SOMETHING
WRONG

13%
I'M HUNGRY

7%
I'M BORED

26%
SOMEONE ELSE DID
SOMETHING WRONG,
and you're being blamed for it

20%
I DID SOMETHING WRONG,
and I'm yelling at you to make it
look like it was your fault

REASONS I'M YELLING AT YOU
A Breakdown

IMs FROM HELL: **THIS HAPPENS**
(More Frequently Than You'd Expect)

12:33 P.M.

BOSS

UGH. My assistant
is being SO
annoying today!!!1!!1

12:33 P.M.

Ummm . . .

ASSISTANT

12:33 P.M.

BOSS

wrong IM window.

12:33 P.M.

BOSS

who do i owe
calls to? get them
on the phone.

12:34 P.M.

OK

ASSISTANT

E-MAILS FROM HELL: **LECTURES**
(Unnecessary)

----

i do not understand why u cant send me things i need on time. i asked for that document by the end of 2day. its now past midnite. the day is officially over. i gave u plenty of time 2 work on it. if u cant do ur job i am going 2 have 2 find someone else. i need someone who is organized and on top of things, like i am.

I'm sorry, but I sent it to you 4 hours ago. Did you not receive my e-mail?

----

theres a typo in the last pargraph. U need to get better at proofreading.

IMs FROM HELL: **MANNERS**
(One-Sided)

10:02 A.M.

BOSS

coffee. black.
splenda.

10:02 A.M.

Coming right up.

ASSISTANT

10:21 A.M.

BOSS

coffee refill

10:21 A.M.

You got it.

ASSISTANT

11:00 A.M.

BOSS

coffee

11:00 A.M.

Sure, I'll grab it as
soon as I've put
this conference
call together.

ASSISTANT

11:00 A.M.

BOSS

ugh. fine.

THE BOSS -O-METER

How My Response to
Different Situations
Can Help You Determine
Exactly How Terrible I Am

YOU FEEL SICK

BEST BOSS EVER	"Oh no! Go home immediately and get some rest! Don't even think about checking your e-mail for the rest of the day."
NORMAL HUMAN BEING	"Oh, I'm sorry. Do you think you can stick it out for the rest of the day? It would be great if you could."
INCONSIDERATE, BUT NOT PURPOSEFULLY CRUEL	"Oh. That sucks."
EVIL	"Get away from me! I CANNOT get sick right now. We have tons of work to do. And stop blowing your nose so much. It's distracting."

YOU HAVEN'T HAD A CHANCE TO EAT ALL DAY, AND IT'S 3 P.M.

BEST BOSS EVER	"Have you had lunch yet? It's late—you must be starving! Here, take £20 and go get something delicious."
NORMAL HUMAN BEING	"You should probably grab something to eat now, while we're not that busy. But don't take too long."
INCONSIDERATE, BUT NOT PURPOSEFULLY CRUEL	[I don't even notice that you haven't eaten.]
EVIL	"I need you to stay at your desk while I go get something to eat with my friend. Don't even think about stepping away for a second—I'm expecting a very important call." [I am not, and you know it, but you also know that I have a habit of calling to make sure you're at the desk when I'm away.]

THE PROJECT YOU'RE WORKING ON IS DUE SOON

BEST BOSS EVER	[Nothing. I trust that you're working as hard as you can to make it the best possible version of what it is.]
NORMAL HUMAN BEING	"Hey, can I get an ETA on that project?"
INCONSIDERATE, BUT NOT PURPOSEFULLY CRUEL	"Hurry up. All this waiting better be worth it."
EVIL	"Are you done yet?" [Asked every five minutes, while pacing a continuous circle around your desk.]

YOU MISSED A PHONE CALL BECAUSE YOU HAD TO GO TO THE BATHROOM

BEST BOSS EVER	[Nothing. I answered the phone myself.]
NORMAL HUMAN BEING	"Where did you go? I had to answer the phone myself."
INCONSIDERATE, BUT NOT PURPOSEFULLY CRUEL	"You missed a call. There's a voice mail. It better not be from someone important."
EVIL	"The only thing you have to do at this job is answer my phones. [Not true.] If you can't do that, what am I paying you all this money for? [I'm not paying you that much money at all.] Go to the bathroom on your own time. [You don't have any of your own time anymore, thanks to me.] Next time this happens, you're fired. [That might actually be a relief.]"

MY PERSONAL LIFE

Welcome to the World of Too Much Information

Your Ears *(Protecting Them)*

I will not talk in a baby voice on the phone to my significant other within your earshot.

Opportunities *(Good and Not Good)*

I will not ask you if you want to earn some extra cash outside of work, saying I have "a great opportunity" for you to do so, which, when you inquire more about it, turns out to be a regular gig on weekends babysitting my spoiled children.

Dry Cleaning *(Foresight)*

I will not send you to the dry cleaner's with two weeks' worth of my laundry, call you on your way there, concerned that there's an "important receipt" in one of the garments, demand that you pull over, dump all my dirty designer clothes out in your backseat, go through the pockets one by one, and then call you again just as you've finished to let you know that actually, I found the receipt in the pocket of the clothes I'm currently wearing.

Failures *(Inevitable)*

I will not accuse you of being a defeatist when you tell me for the fourth and final time that no, there is no way an intern can go to the DVLA to get my "stolen" driver's license replaced.

Moving *(Understatements)*

I will not ask if you can help me move "some stuff" over the weekend, only for you to show up in your ten-year-old Ford Fiesta to discover that by "some stuff" I mean "almost all of my stuff," because I'm fighting with my significant other and, though I am rich enough to stay in a five-star hotel instead of on the couch, don't want to pay for professional movers.

My Love Life *(Keeping It to Myself)*

I will not ask you to create an account for me on a dating website. I will not ask you to create an account for me on a site that hooks younger women up with sugar daddies. I will not ask you to create an account for me on a site that connects married people with other married people who want to discreetly cheat on their spouses. If I want to indulge in this kind of activity, I'll do it myself on my own time.

Themed Birthday Parties *(Planning)*

If I decide that I want to have a Magic Mike–themed birthday party involving male strippers, I won't make you organize the whole thing, eventually causing our IT department to shut down your computer due to the suddenly inappropriate nature of your Google searches.

Documents *(TMI)*

If I need you to reprint something for me, I'll just ask you to reprint it. I will not, however, sidle up to your desk, ask you to reprint it, explain that I "left it on [person you've never heard of's] bedside table when I snuck out this morning, so I don't think I'll be getting that back," and then try to high-five you.

Tanning *(Fake)*

I will not ask you to try out my new fake tanner on your arm, because I'm worried it might turn me orange.

Dinner Parties *(Fake Cooking for)*

I will not make you spend three hours in rush-hour traffic driving all over town to pick up take-out dishes from various restaurants that I will then assemble into a "homemade dinner" for the party I'm hosting that night.

Shopping (Futile)

I will not make you spend two months tracking down an obscure French cologne that is not sold in the United States and then, when you triumphantly present me with what seems to be the last bottle in existence, say, "Oh. I switched to a different brand last month when you couldn't find it. Didn't I tell you?"

Dating (Scheduling)

Your responsibilities as my assistant will not include scheduling dates for me with five different people in five different cities, while making sure none of them finds out about the others.

Polite Questions (TMI)

When you politely ask, "How are you?" while rolling calls first thing in the morning, I will reply with no more than a sentence, and will probably just say, "Fine, thanks." I will not, however, reel off a list of all the problems I'm having in my personal life and describe how they make me feel, detail the strange and disturbing methods my new-wave therapist recommends, and then end with "So I guess I'm fine, thanks."

Baby Showers (Planning)

If I need to have a conference call with some of my friends to plan a baby shower, I might ask you for help setting up a dial-in, but I won't make you listen to the entire ninety-minute conversation. And take detailed notes.

Your Job Description

(Limits of)

I will never ask you to polish my shoes. You're an assistant, not a butler. (Butlers get paid a lot more.)

Errands (Unforgivable)

I will not ask you to go to my house on a weekend to collect a stool sample from my dog and take it to the vet, because "I'm too busy" playing eighteen holes of golf with my mates.

Knowledge *(Using Mine)*

I will not make you handle all the details of the estate tax on my dead relative's belongings, remaining completely unhelpful throughout the entire three-month process even though I have a law degree, you have a B.A. in film theory, and the relative is someone I've been close to since birth but have never even mentioned to you.

Baby Showers
(Responsibility Without Reward)

When my friends have them, you will not be responsible for picking up the thirty-pound cake emblazoned with their baby pictures at 9 A.M. on a Sunday.

Invites *(Ulterior Motives)*

I will not invite you to a "fun cocktail party" at my home and then, when you show up with a bottle of the nicest wine you can afford, reveal that I really need you there to keep my kids under control, since the sitter bailed on me that morning.

My Kids *(School Projects)*

I will never make you spend a weekend handcrafting and signing fifty valentines for my child's nursery class. I will never make you do my child's maths homework and then get mad at you when he gets an A instead of an A+. I will never make you spend a Thursday night constructing a papier-mâché volcano for my child's science class the next day. Helping my kid cheat is my job, not yours.

Excuses *(Contagious)*

After you tell me that a colleague had to cancel a meeting due to his dog being sick, I will not then suddenly "remember" that my dog is sick, too, and try to use it as an excuse for the temper tantrum I threw at you that morning.

Dog-Sitting *(Extensions)*

I will not ask you to take care of my dog "just for a weekend," which then turns into a full month, "because I'm just too busy right now, and he really likes you!"

Errands *(Awkward)*

I will not send you out to buy me new underwear.

Event Planning
(Counterproductive)

I will not call you into my office, interrupting your work on a very important and time-sensitive project, so I can ask your opinion on different kinds of napkins for my friend's hen party, advice which I will then disregard to the point of making sure to pick your last choice.

Professionalism
(Uncomfortable Breaches of)

I will not fight with my significant other in front of you.

My Kids *(Unnecessary Details About)*

I will not describe to you, in detail, the various stages of my child's potty training, with a status update every morning.

My Past *(Should Stay There)*

When a picture of someone I slept with in the past shows up on a blog or in a newspaper, I will not call you into my office, point to the picture, and brag about it.

Secrets *(Keeping Them to Myself)*

I will not use you as my personal gossip confidant, telling you everything about all of my friends—who's sleeping with whom, who's cheating on a significant other, who's planning to leave whose spouse—so that every time you meet these friends you're reduced to an awkward, fumbling mess as you try not to reveal that you know exactly what terrible people they really are.

Overheard Conversations
(Unsettling)

You will never overhear me say to a friend on the phone, "Well, I haven't broken [him or her] in yet," only to realize that I'm talking not about you, my new assistant, but, even worse, about my new boyfriend or girlfriend.

My Household Staff
(Forced Management of)

I will not make you act as a supervisor to my housekeeper, who is twenty years older than you, makes much more money than you do, and finds your attempts to communicate with her in broken Spanish hilarious, because I feel guilty about telling her she did something wrong, but oddly not guilty about yelling at you every day.

My Kids *(Forced Babysitting)*

When my kids come to visit me at the office, I will not hang out with them for five minutes and then encourage them to go play with "Auntie/Uncle Assistant!"— leaving you to supervise them for an hour while you place fifty phone calls for me.

Lists *(Awkward)*

I will not ask you to compile a list of the best divorce lawyers in town, "quietly," especially when you and my spouse deal with each other on a daily basis and actually have a pretty friendly relationship.

Sympathy *(Backfiring)*

I will not complain to you about my significant other and then, when you try to sympathize with me, accuse you of insulting him or her.

Taste in Music *(Expectation Versus Reality)*

I will not make you create a playlist full of "hip music" for the party I'm having at my house over the weekend, and then get mad at you when you fill it with cool indie rock instead of Rihanna, Lady Gaga, Beyoncé, and Britney Spears, who are apparently the only modern musicians I've ever heard of.

Mannequins

(Treating You Like One)

After discovering that we have the same shoe size/jacket size/dress size, I will not ask you to go to a store on your lunch break, try on a number of items of clothing, photograph yourself in them, and then wait there for me to decide which I want you to buy and bring back to me.

Your Opinion *(Apparent Value of)*

I will not ask if you'll "take a look at something for me and give me your opinion," which you excitedly say yes to, happy to finally reach the stage in your career where you get to have some input, only for me to e-mail you my teenager's coursework on Dante's *Inferno*.

Shopping Trips *(Involuntary)*

If I decide to go shopping during lunch, I won't make you come with me so you can tell me whether or not I look fat in a certain outfit.

8%
DEFLECTING
small but surprisingly
heavy objects thrown
at you when you have
to go to my house for
some reason

5%
OVERHEARING
my teenager scream,
"I hate you!" at me,
and suppressing a
satisfied smile

9%
**EXPLAINING THAT
MUMMY/DADDY**
can't come to the phone right
now because she/he is "in a
meeting" (napping)

16%
FREE BABYSITTING
that I tricked you into doing

42%
BUYING THEM THINGS
that you would never be
able to afford for yourself

20%
EXTENSIVELY "PROOFREADING" AND "EDITING"
their homework and/or UCAS forms

YOUR INTERACTIONS WITH MY KIDS
A Breakdown

WHY MY KIDS HAVE IT BETTER NOW THAN YOU EVER WILL

WHAT YOU BOUGHT FOR MY KIDS	WHAT YOU BOUGHT FOR YOURSELF
Insulated lunch bags in five different colors, one for each day of the week **£75.00**	Plastic bag left over from grocery shopping **£0.00**
Barbie Three-Story Dream House **£480.00**	A bottle of whiskey **£21.99**

WHAT YOU BOUGHT FOR MY KIDS

Hideous designer backpack

£795.00

One month of gourmet, premade dinners tailored for kids

£450.00

The Complete *Star Wars* Blu-Ray set

£140.00

A kid-sized electric version of my BMW convertible

£250.00

New iPad

£629.00

WHAT YOU BOUGHT FOR YOURSELF

Free promotional linen tote bag

£0.00

---

36 packages of ramen noodles

£17.95

Your parents' Netflix Instant account password

£0.00

A much-needed oil change

£30.00

New iPhone charger to replace the one I "borrowed" indefinitely

£29.00

BOSS
WRANGLING
FOR BEGINNERS

Questions I Might Ask You at Some Point (and How to Answer Them)

QUESTION	WRONG ANSWER	RIGHT ANSWER
"Do you like this shirt/chair/dog/pillow/book/poster/rug/hat/hideously expensive piece of artwork that I'm thinking of buying?"	"It's nice, but I think…"	"Yes! It's great!"
	WHY IT'S WRONG: Now you have to explain why you don't like it, and no matter what you say, I'll take it as an insult to my taste. Best to just let me make a terrible shopping decision.	**WHY IT'S RIGHT:** That's all you have to say. Now you can get back to work.

QUESTION	WRONG ANSWER	RIGHT ANSWER
"What would you do in my situation?"	"[honest assessment of the situation followed by logical and sound suggestions of what I might consider doing]"	"[facial expression of deep thought followed by vague words of concern and encouragement]"
	WHY IT'S WRONG: I will almost certainly misunderstand what you are trying to tell me, act on this "advice" that I think you've given me, and then blame you when it turns out badly.	**WHY IT'S RIGHT:** If you don't give me any concrete advice, I can't screw it up, and at least I'll see you as supportive, if not insightful.
"Should I get a new car?"	"Yes/No"	"Do you want a new car?"
	WHY IT'S WRONG: I want a new car, but I don't want to be told that I should or shouldn't get one. All this answer will do is drag the conversation out for another 15 minutes as I argue against whatever position you've taken.	**WHY IT'S RIGHT:** Appealing to my greed is the best way to get me to come to a decision as quickly as possible. The answer will be "yes," though I might take a second to wax nostalgic about my old car for appearance's sake.
"What should I get for lunch?"	"[something from the place that's the easiest to order from and takes the shortest amount of time to get here]"	"[something from the place that's the hardest to order from and takes the longest amount of time to get here]"
	WHY IT'S WRONG: There's no way I'm going to order anything you suggest to me.	**WHY IT'S RIGHT:** I might not order from the fastest place, but at least I won't order from the slowest one either.

YOUR PERSONAL LIFE

If You're Even Allowed to Have One

Privacy *(Respecting Yours)*

I will not peer over your shoulder as you're eating lunch at your desk, point to a random event in your personal calendar, and ask, "What's that?"

Postholiday Comments

(Unnecessary)

After going through the motions of caring about how your holidays were, I will not then remark, with a noticeable amount of glee, that you look "well rested and well fed."

Compliments *(Confusing)*

I will not make a habit of frequently complimenting totally mundane pieces of your wardrobe in a bright, fake tone of voice, to the point where you're not even sure if you like what you're wearing anymore.

Betrayals *(Casual)*

If I overhear you telling an annoying coworker that you're completely slammed with work tonight and therefore can't join him for happy hour at the terrible bar down the street, I will not say loudly, "What are you talking about? You don't have anything to do for me tonight."

Help (Unwanted)

I will not offer you completely unsolicited skin-care advice involving a regimen that costs more per week than you make every two days.

Family (Importance of)

If you ask if you can take an extra day off before Christmas so you can spend more time visiting your family on the other side of the country, whom you see maybe three times a year because you can't afford to fly more frequently, I will not reply, "Why? Isn't three days enough?"

Lunch (Yours)

When you actually have somewhere to be during lunch and for the first time in five months can't spend the hour eating at your desk and printing out documents for me when I forward them to you, I won't take thirty minutes to decide whether or not you can leave and then, when I begrudgingly say yes, immediately ask, "You'll be back at exactly two P.M., right?"

Weight (Yours)

I won't comment on it unless you do. When you do hint that you're feeling fat, I'll say, "Stop being stupid. You look great," since I know that any overeating you've done recently is probably my fault.

Weight (Mine)

I will not ask you how much you weigh and, after you reluctantly answer, sigh in relief and say, "Well, that makes me feel better."

Compliments (Taking Them Back)

When I compliment you on a piece of clothing, and you proudly tell me you got it for £5 at a thrift store, I will admire your resourcefulness rather than making a face that suggests a piece of crap is stuck to your arm.

Your Birthday (False Hope)

I will remember your birthday and hand you a gift. I will not forget your birthday and hand you an envelope with a cheque inside—payable to me—that I will then ask you to drive to my bank and deposit.

Significant Others *(Insulting Yours)*

After spending a scant five minutes making small talk with your significant other at the office holiday party, I will not loudly ask you the next day, "Why are you dating that loser anyway?"

Snooping *(Unashamedly)*

When you run to the bathroom, you won't return to find me rifling through the papers on your desk, looking completely blasé and not at all guilty when you catch me.

Advice *(Unsound)*

I will not frequently offer you dating and relationship advice, especially since I haven't been able to hold on to a relationship for more than two weeks during the time you've worked for me.

Remarks on Genealogy *(Confusingly Insulting)*

When your parents come to visit, and you bring them into the office for a quick tour, I will not remark the next day that "now I understand where you came from."

After-Work Activities *(Intrusions on)*

When you tell me you have plans to go to a movie tonight, I will not exclaim, "Oh! I've been wanting to see that!" and make you find me tickets for the same screening you're going to.

Your Birthday Party *(Invitations to)*

I won't get mad at you for not inviting me to your birthday party, even though I'm twenty-five years older than you, married with kids, and wouldn't be caught dead at the bar where you've decided to hold it.

Questions *(Creepy)*

When I call you on the weekend to ask you a question or tell you something I need you to do, I won't first ask, "What are you doing right now?" in some kind of strange attempt to be considerate that instead just ends up making both of us feel awkward while you reluctantly reveal the details of your normal, boring life.

Middle Schoolers
(Behaving Like One)

I will not eavesdrop while you talk on the phone with your parents during your lunch break, and then later make fun of you for telling them "I love you," as if I'm a thirteen-year-old boy.

Time Management *(Forced)*

A few months after you've started working for me, I will not inquire as to what your hobbies outside of work are and, after you list them, say, "Yeah, you're going to have to stop all of those. They take up way too much time." Especially if you've just told me that you like reading, watching movies, and running.

Packages
(Unwanted Inspections of)

When you get things that you've ordered online delivered to the office so they won't get stolen from outside your apartment door, I will not appear beside your desk at the first sounds of ripping tape, watch you open the package, and then say in dismay, "What's that?!?" when it becomes clear that it's not for me, forcing you to awkwardly explain that the thirty-six-pack of ramen noodles is actually a little cheaper on Amazon than it is in stores.

Facebook Stalking *(Blatant)*

When you walk into my office to drop some papers on my desk, you will not catch me in the act of scrolling through your Facebook pictures, which I won't even act ashamed about.

Personal Conversations
(Reciprocity)

I will not spend a good ten minutes talking to you about something fun I did over the weekend and then, when you try to tell me an equally interesting story about your life, walk away from you when you're mid-sentence, exclaiming, "Well, back to work!" as if we had finished the conversation together.

Hints *(Not-So-Subtle)*

You will not walk into the office one morning to find a bottle of prescription dandruff shampoo sitting on the corner of your desk, which I will say "I got this just for you!" with a big, generous smile on my face.

Your Neighborhood
(Snap Judgments)

If I ask what part of town you live in, I will not then make a scared face at your answer, saying, "Ohhhhhhhhhhh, there. Well, it must be cheap at least."

Advice (Not Applicable)

I will not try to give you investment and money-management tips, when the amount I'm paying you is barely enough for you to invest in rent and food.

Segues (Natural but Uncalled for)

I will not turn a casual conversation about the music of the Beatles into an in-depth interrogation about whether you've ever done drugs.

Assumptions (Based on Appearance)

I will not act surprised when you reveal that you have plans to go to a few parties over the weekend, explaining that I thought you were "a prude," due to the clothes you wear to work, which are admittedly pretty boring, but no more boring than anyone else's in our very conservative, corporate office.

Weeknights (Hypocrisy)

I will not call you on your mobile after work hours and start ranting about an e-mail I need you to send right away, and then, when you explain that you're actually out to dinner, ask, "On a weeknight?!" acting appalled at your lack of work ethic, even though you spend at least one day every month making up fake business-related dinner meetings for me so I can expense my many weeknight dinners (often take-out) to the company.

Nutrition (Unwanted Advice on)

I will not peer over your shoulder as you're writing down your grocery list at the end of the day and comment, "You shouldn't eat so much cheese—it's terrible for you."

Suggestions (from a Rich Person)

I will not make you video chat with me from home over the weekend so "we can talk face-to-face," and then, as our conversation is wrapping up, suggest that you donate your "ratty old couch" to Goodwill and buy yourself a new one, even though you just got it a year ago and the only reason I'm calling it ratty is because I can tell it's from IKEA.

Your Hair *(Incorrect Assumptions About)*

I will not comment that "it looks like it's time to get your roots dyed," when you don't even dye your hair at all.

Therapy *(Causing the Need for More of)*

I won't make jokes about how working for me is going to drive you into therapy, when it has in fact already done that, which I know about, since you leave the office at 7 P.M. sharp every Tuesday to make it to your sessions.

Surprise *(Insulting)*

After you've worked for me for six months, I won't finally ask, awkwardly, if you have a boyfriend or girlfriend, and then if you say yes, reply, "You do?!" with an expression of genuine surprise on my face.

Personal Questions *(Only Allowed from Me)*

I will not ask all kinds of probing, uncomfortable questions about your childhood, parents, siblings, and school days, but then snap, "That's personal!" whenever you try to engage me in conversation about the same topics in my life.

Assumptions *(Financial)*

I will not assume that your parents are giving you money every month and, when you reveal that they're not, express surprise that you're actually able to live off the measly salary I'm paying you.

Personality Tests *(Not Always the Most Accurate)*

I will not decide that I know exactly who you are and what your personality is based solely on your astrological sign.

IMs FROM HELL: CURIOSITY
(Insulting)

BOSS — 4:33 P.M.
what are you doing this weekend?

4:33 P.M.
Me? — **ASSISTANT**

BOSS — 4:34 P.M.
Y

4:34 P.M.
I'm going to a BBQ on Saturday and then we're going to a movie on Sunday night, I think. — **ASSISTANT**

BOSS — 4:35 P.M.
who's "we"?

4:35 P.M.
Some friends and me. — **ASSISTANT**

BOSS — 4:35 P.M.
oh good

BOSS — 4:36 P.M.
im glad you have friends

BOSS — 4:37 P.M.
i wasn't really sure you did

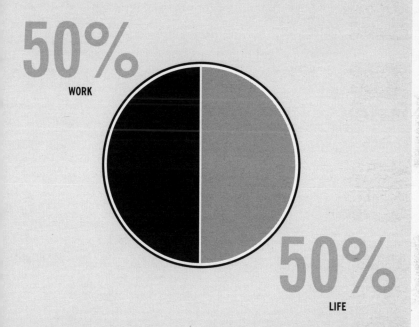

50% **WORK**

50% **LIFE**

YOUR IDEA OF YOUR PERFECT WORK-LIFE BALANCE
A Breakdown

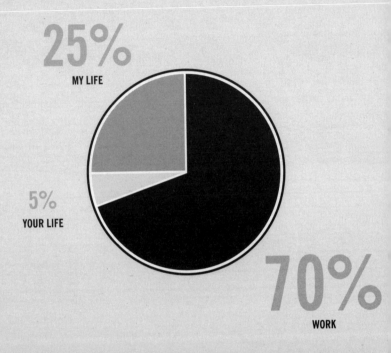

25%
MY LIFE

5%
YOUR LIFE

70%
WORK

MY IDEA OF YOUR PERFECT WORK-LIFE BALANCE
A Breakdown

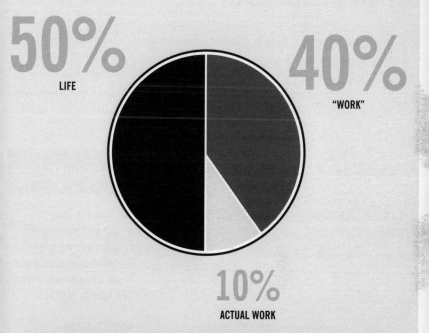

50%
LIFE

40%
"WORK"

10%
ACTUAL WORK

MY IDEA OF MY PERFECT WORK-LIFE BALANCE
A Breakdown

BOSS
WRANGLING
FOR BEGINNERS

More Questions I Might Ask You at Some Point (and How to Answer Them)

QUESTION	WRONG ANSWER	RIGHT ANSWER
"What are you doing this weekend?"	"I don't really have any plans."	"Oh, well, I'm going to brunch with some friends on Saturday, then maybe the beach or a museum and then a birthday party after that, then on Sunday…"
	WHY IT'S WRONG: You will now be working for me all weekend.	**WHY IT'S RIGHT:** I'm bored by this point, but also aware that you are not available to cater to my every whim.

QUESTION	WRONG ANSWER	RIGHT ANSWER
"What's your favorite bar around here?"	"[name of your favorite bar around here]"	"[name of your fourth-favorite bar around here]"
	WHY IT'S WRONG: Now you might run into me there.	**WHY IT'S RIGHT:** You can still go to your favorite bar, which was probably too cool for me to enjoy anyway.
"Do you like kids?"	"Yes!/Not really."	"I like them, but I'm not very good with them."
	WHY IT'S WRONG: Now I see you as either my new babysitter or a psychopath.	**WHY IT'S RIGHT:** You're not a psychopath, but you're not my new babysitter either.
"Where did you get that shirt?"	"Target"	"Bloomingdale's"
	WHY IT'S WRONG: You've turned an almost-compliment into ammunition for a follow-up insult.	**WHY IT'S RIGHT:** If I was interested in it, I already thought it came from there to begin with, plus, you might get the added bonus of me spending a weekday afternoon there, trying to find the same one, instead of bothering you at the office.

IN SICKNESS AND IN HEALTH

Together Forever (at Least That's What It Feels Like)

Accusations *(Absurd)*

I will not accuse you of having bedbugs just because you managed to get a mosquito bite on your arm during winter.

Doctor's Appointments

(Paranoia)

I will not accuse you of sneaking away for an interview when you ask for time off to go to the doctor, even though I've been telling you to "get away from me" all week due to your snuffly nose and hacking cough.

Sickness *(Effects of)*

When you let me know that you're sick on Monday, I will not tell you that "we have to make it through this week," and

then spend the rest of the week saying to you every few hours, "What is wrong with you this week? Get it together!"

Sick Days *(Missing the Point of)*

When you tell me you're going home sick for the second half of the day, I won't say, "Oh! Perfect!" and assign you a hugely tedious and exhausting research and/or data entry project to do, "now that you have some time on your hands."

Stomach Flu *(Side Effects of)*

If you e-mail me to say you have a stomach flu and won't be able to come in that day, I won't reply, "I love stomach flus! They make you skinny!"

"Oh. We all thought it was probably just gas."

Sympathy
(Appropriate Expression of)

When you e-mail me to say you're sick and not able to come to work, I'll reply, "Get better," and maybe even send a delivery of soup to your apartment. I will not ignore your e-mails completely and then spend the next day making passive-aggressive comments about how I thought you'd quit.

Bragging *(Unearned)*

I will not brag to my colleagues about the fact that, when you had a severe case of bronchitis, you still came in to work every morning for a half day, especially since you did so not out of any kind of loyalty or passion for the job but out of fear of being fired.

Assumptions *(Insulting)*

When you have to leave work early one day due to severe stomach pains, and later e-mail me to say that you had to get your appendix removed, I won't reply,

Contagion *(Forced)*

I will not insist that you work a full day at the office when you're clearly suffering from a terrible cold, and then get mad at you for "infecting me" when I catch the same cold a few days later, which most likely would not have happened had I not made you work in close proximity to me for a ten-hour day.

Accusations *(Insulting)*

When you call in sick on a Friday morning, I won't immediately accuse you of having a hangover, especially if this is the first sick day you've taken in the two years you've worked for me.

Signatures *(Obnoxious)*

When you break a bone that requires you to wear a cast for a few weeks, I won't insist that I be able to sign it, and print my name in all caps on a very visible part of it, as if I'm branding you like cattle, and not even bother to add something like "Get well soon."

Antibiotics *(Importance of)*

I won't insist on self-medicating with various homeopathic remedies when I'm sick, ignoring the fact that my doctor has prescribed me a course of antibiotics, and then get everyone in the office sick because my contagious illness has now lasted six weeks instead of the one it would've taken for the antibiotics to make it go away.

Sick Days *(Arbitrary)*

I won't insist on continuing to work at the office when I have a bad cold, which will almost definitely spread to you, but use a headache as an excuse to take a day off when I just don't feel like going to work.

Allergies and Colds
(Difference Between)

I will not accuse you of being sick when you just have allergies, and of just having allergies when you're actually sick.

Medication *(Disgusting)*

When you come in to work with a slight cold, I will not insist that you try my weird homeopathic medicine, which consists of pills the size of a finger joint that taste like grass mixed with mothballs.

Supplies *(Depleting Them)*

I will not take all of the Nurofen out of the office first aid kit to deal with my constant stress headaches, so when you actually need it, there isn't any left.

Healthy Meals
(Inconsistency)

I will not make you go out of your way each morning to pick up a special egg-white omelet (which tastes like nothing) for my breakfast and then send you to McDonald's for my lunch.

Workout Suggestions
(Exorbitant)

After I start working out with a new personal trainer, I will not enthusiastically suggest that "you should give him a try!" even though we both know I'm paying him more per month than I'm paying you.

Sneezing *(Real Causes of)*

I will not douse myself with so much perfume or cologne that you have to stifle a sneeze every time you come into my office, causing me to wonder out loud, "Why are you so sickly all the time?"

Head Scratching
(Assumptions About)

If I catch you literally scratching your head in confusion at one of my more incoherent e-mails, I will not accuse you of having lice.

Requests
(Completely Unnecessary)

I will not insist that you feel my biceps after a workout session.

Hints *(Insulting)*

I will not give you a year-long membership to the gym in our office building, including in your Christmas card the brochure with the "Weight Loss Specialists" section circled aggressively in biro.

Dentistry *(Results of)*

I will not insist on working through the rest of the day after I have a root canal in the morning, the combination of painkillers and swelling making my words completely incomprehensible, rather than their normal level of mostly incomprehensible.

Blood Sugar *(Importance of Maintaining Proper Levels)*

I will not decide to go on a fad diet that involves severe caloric restriction, so that my blood sugar dips way below normal several times during the day, causing me to have even more tantrums, yelling fits, and pointless arguments than usual, all directed at you, of course.

Salads *(Excessive Precision)*

I will not make you count out an exact number of lettuce leaves, nuts, dried fruit, tiny cubes of cheese, and rings of olives when you're putting together my "healthy" salad for lunch, and freak out if I think you're over or under, though I wouldn't know, since I've never actually counted out forty leaves of baby spinach myself.

Exercise *(Forced)*

If I'm feeling sluggish at around 3 P.M., I will not force you to go on an "energy jog" with me around the office, the result of which will be only to make you feel like a complete fool in front of everyone.

Team Sports
(Memories of PE)

If our company has a mandatory team-building day once a year that involves rounders, I will pick you for my team, rather than leaving you to be the last one to be picked, and then choosing you with a great show of reluctance, just because you once told me you had asthma as a child.

Health Drinks *(Hard-to-Find)*

I will not make you spend an entire workday driving to every Whole Foods in the city, trying to find my favorite live-culture "green drink," which looks and tastes exactly like fermented grass steeped in water and expires within a few days, making you unable to buy more than three at a time.

Yoga *(Not-So-Calming)*

I will not do yoga in my office during lunch (sitar music, incense, chanting, and all) and, every day, invite you to join me.

Naps *(for Me, Not for You)*

I will not insist that the forty-five-minute "power naps" I take almost daily are for my mental health, but snap at you if you ever look less than fully awake or fail to completely hide a yawn from me.

Overheard Recommendations
(Not the Same as Invitations)

After I overhear you recommending your gym to a coworker, I will not decide to give it a try and start working out there at the exact same time you do, so that you're forced to watch me pant on a treadmill in less-than-flattering workout gear in the one place that was your refuge from office-related stress.

Stress *(Causing)*

I will not give you a gift certificate to an acupuncturist for your birthday, insisting that "it'll help relieve some of your stress" (failing to mention that I am the main cause of that stress), even though every time I've recommended acupuncture to you, you've told me that you're completely terrified of needles.

Theories *(Strange and Exhausting)*

I will not take up most of your lunch break describing to you the invisible mold that grows in your body when you eat sugar, and all of its ill effects, and explaining that that's why I'm not eating sugar at all these days, and why I have so much more energy, and can't you really tell the difference?

Medical Translation *(Not Part of Your Job)*

I will not hand you test results from my doctor and say, "See if you can figure out what these mean." No matter what they mean, it's going to be more information than you wanted.

Sick Days *(Suggested Versus Requested)*

I will not insist that you take a day off when you have a slight cold, trying to play the nice boss for once, since "we don't have that much to do today anyway," and then, when you come down with a serious illness later that month and actually ask for a sick day, say, "Another one?!" and give you a disapproving look.

Offers *(Seemingly Generous, Actually Unhelpful)*

When you pull a muscle in your back, I will not offer to "send you to my chiropractor" if I actually mean "give you his number so you can call and make an appointment" but not "take care of his three-hundred-dollar bill for thirty minutes of work," since it's the ten hours a day you spend sitting in your office chair that caused the problem.

Requests *(Very Uncomfortable)*

I will not ask you to feel my forehead if I think I have a fever. I'll send you out to buy a thermometer instead, to save us both the experience of having your hand pressed up against my sweaty skin.

Medical Degrees
(Nontransferable)

I will not act offended if you seek a professional's opinion when you're sick, instead of relying on my diagnosis, which I insist is correct because "my uncle was a doctor."

Workouts
(Reliving Them, Awkwardly)

After a workout with my trainer, I will not spend half an hour detailing to you all the things he or she made me do and how that made me feel.

Lunch *(Efficiency Versus Flavor)*

When you ask if you can step away for a minute to grab some lunch, I will not toss one of my wet-cardboard-flavored "energy" bars at you and say, "Here. Have a free lunch on me. It's good for you!"

Unhealthy Consumption
(Proven and Unproven)

I will not lecture you almost every day about all the toxins you put into your body by consuming cheese/ meat/ Diet Coke/nonorganic foods/ gluten/sugar, but still go outside every lunch break to smoke my daily cigarette.

IMs FROM HELL: DIAGNOSES
(Incorrect)

11:06 A.M.

 BOSS

I need you to get an intern to pick me up some Lemsip, tissues, and throat lozenges. The honey lemon kind.

11:07 A.M.

Of course. Are you not feeling well? **ASSISTANT**

11:08 A.M.

 BOSS

allergies

11:09 A.M.

Claritin might actually be better for allergies than Lemsip. **ASSISTANT**

11:10 A.M.

 BOSS

lemsip

11:15 A.M.

 BOSS

the strongest kind like what they use to make meth

11:15 A.M.

OK **ASSISTANT**

11:20 A.M.

 BOSS

can you please come empty my trash can? it's full of tissues. also pls make me a cup of tea

15%

AN ACTUAL, SERIOUS ILLNESS
that I still don't believe you have, even though you've sent me a doctor's note

17%

YOU HAVE A JOB INTERVIEW,
and you've used up all your doctor's appointment excuses on actual doctor's appointments

7%

"FOOD POISONING,"
aka really really bad hangover

7%

THE THOUGHT OF COMING TO WORK
is literally making you sick to your stomach

12%

I MADE YOU WORK ALL WEEKEND,
so you're taking today off to make up for it

42%

I WAS SICK
but refused to stay home or take medication, and now you have what I had

REASONS YOU'RE OFF SICK
A Breakdown

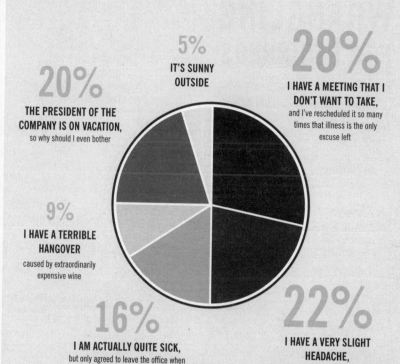

5%
IT'S SUNNY
OUTSIDE

28%
I HAVE A MEETING THAT I
DON'T WANT TO TAKE,
and I've rescheduled it so many
times that illness is the only
excuse left

20%
THE PRESIDENT OF THE
COMPANY IS ON VACATION,
so why should I even bother

9%
I HAVE A TERRIBLE
HANGOVER
caused by extraordinarily
expensive wine

16%
I AM ACTUALLY QUITE SICK,
but only agreed to leave the office when
the head of the company told me to

22%
I HAVE A VERY SLIGHT
HEADACHE,
but refuse to take painkillers "because
they're so bad for your liver"

REASONS I'M OFF SICK
A Breakdown

BOSS
WRANGLING
FOR BEGINNERS

*Should You Stay Home Sick
(How to Decide)*

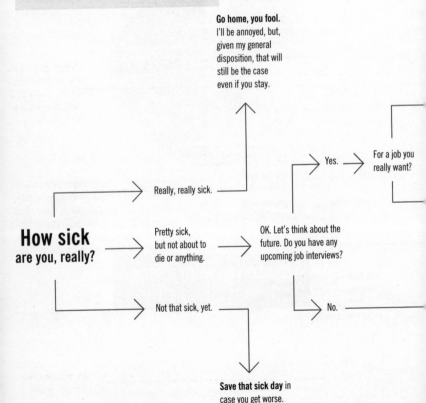

Go home, you fool.
I'll be annoyed, but,
given my general
disposition, that will
still be the case
even if you stay.

Yes. → For a job you
really want?

Really, really sick. ─

How sick
are you, really?

Pretty sick,
but not about to
die or anything. →

OK. Let's think about the
future. Do you have any
upcoming job interviews?

Not that sick, yet. ─

No. ─

Save that sick day in
case you get worse.

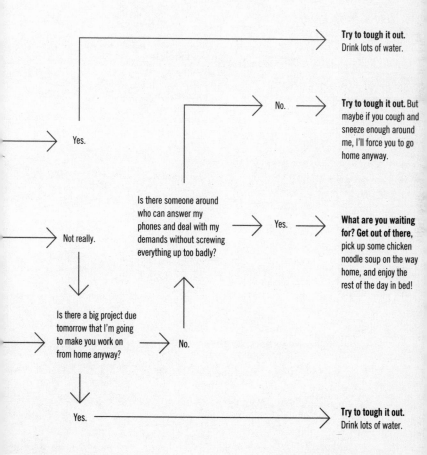

Try to tough it out.
Drink lots of water.

No. → **Try to tough it out.** But
maybe if you cough and
sneeze enough around
me, I'll force you to go
home anyway.

Yes. →

Is there someone around
who can answer my
phones and deal with my
demands without screwing
everything up too badly? → Yes. → **What are you waiting
for? Get out of there,**
pick up some chicken
noodle soup on the way
home, and enjoy the
rest of the day in bed!

Not really.

Is there a big project due
tomorrow that I'm going
to make you work on
from home anyway? → No.

Yes. → **Try to tough it out.**
Drink lots of water.

OKAY, YOU CAN GO HOME NOW

Well, dear future assistant, this should give you a head start, but don't become too complacent. As long as there are bosses with assistants in this world, there will always be another sneaky, psychologically devastating, or just plain annoying form of torture around the corner. So stay vigilant. Stay calm. Stay smart. And stay away from tequila shots on weeknights and karaoke at office Christmas parties.

You can do it.

ACKNOWLEDGMENTS

I would like to thank:

Erin Malone, Ashley Fox, and Erin Conroy, for their wisdom.

Anna Thompson, for her invaluable input.

Abbe Ertel Magid, for understanding everything I say.

Annie Connors, Nicky Loomis, Lolly O'Fallon, and Lindsey Ramey, for their undying emotional support.

My parents, for everything.

My past bosses, for being good sports. I hope.

Everyone who has been, will be, or still is an assistant, for the strength it takes to hold out just one more day before quitting. Just one more day. That's all.

ABOUT THE AUTHOR

LYDIA WHITLOCK graduated from Yale in 2008 with a degree in Film Studies and moved to L.A. with the hopes of making it big in showbiz, bolstered by the belief that she was special, which can be blamed entirely on her parents. Instead, she found herself working as a Hollywood assistant, where her experiences inspired her to create the popular blog ToMyAssistant.com.